SECRETS REVEALED

YOUR STORY

TERRENCE LEE TALLEY

For information, please contact:

www.ten16press.com
Waukesha, WI

Cover and interior design by Kaeley Dunteman
Stock imagery provided by unsplash.com
Unsplash Contributors: annie-spratt, freestocks, lindsay-henwood, dave-adamson, filip-kominik, lacie-slezak, nicole-geri-ohK, ihor-malytskyi, debby-hudson, kelly-sikkema, tim-goedhart, bruno-nasciment, fab-lentz, ian-rX12B5uX7Q, volkan-olmez, nicola-fioravanti, nevin-ruttanabo, and priscilla-du-preez

FOR BULK ORDERS OR WHOLESALE DISCOUNTS:
Contact Shannon Ishizaki
shannon@orangehatpublishing.com | 414-212-5477

Here's the deal: you either bought, were given, or chose this book to look at, so thank you for that. Or if you are being forced to go through it, I hope it turns out better than you expect. If it makes you feel any better, this book has pictures in it. No matter what brought you here, I am glad to have you.

Before you read this book, though, there are some rules you have to follow. First rule: THERE ARE NO RULES! Below are some suggestions on how to look at this book, but by no means is this a normal book (hence the suggestions). So go crazy.

1. *Do whatever you want with this book.* Read it however you want to read it. Start in the middle, back, front, wherever. If you want to start on page 11, feel free to. It might be weird, but go for it. It's your book, so who am I to tell you what to do with it?

2. *Watch your fingers and be careful.* This book is made for people of all ages. You're going to have the opportunity to cut pages, take out pages, and color pages. So if you choose to participate, watch your fingers when using those scissors.

3. *This is not just a book.* I like to think of it more like a journal. It's meant to get you thinking about your story and give you an opportunity to put it on paper. So if you want to let somebody read it later, they'll be able to understand you and your story better. Or if it's for your eyes only, someday this will be a mirror for you to look back on yourself and your story.

That's it. I always had a hard time trying to write about my story, so I just want to help in journaling yours. Hopefully this book makes it a little easier for all of us.

Generally, parents want to give their kids more opportunities than they had, to build a better life for them. I don't know if you have great parents, okay parents, or parents that are not able to be there for you…but I just want to make sure you know that there are people who want to provide a better life for you, even if you don't know them. And since you are surrounded by a cloud of people cheering you on from afar, you can throw off that weight of shame and doubt and run forward in this race called life. A race I know you can win. A race that you can talk about, work through, and reveal in these pages.

Let's get started!

SOMETIMES IT'S THE JOURNEY THAT TEACHES YOU A LOT ABOUT YOUR DESTINATION.

Drake

DON'T GIVE UP
Coping with Depression and Suicide

In this chapter, you'll be following the story of Maggie, a fourteen-year-old struggling with depression. Throughout the chapter, you'll hear Maggie's story about her father's suicide, her feelings of loneliness, and how she deals with these in her everyday life.

We All Have Our Battles

I am not a real athletic guy, but the sport I had some type of talent in was wrestling. I loved the thought of just going out there on my own and doing battle with someone. Winning was the best feeling. When you pin someone and the referee holds up your hand pronouncing you the winner in front of everyone, it's awesome. For someone like me who felt hardly noticed, it was nice to be seen as a winner.

But when I would get pinned down in front of everyone, it was horrible. I'd be on my back in some kind of uncomfortable position, looking at everyone and feeling like they were as embarrassed by me as I was. When the count was done, I would have to pull myself up off the mat, just wanting to never get back on it again.

You might not be physically wrestling, but some of us are wrestling with our past and a losing record. Or maybe you see the battle ahead and are feeling like you already lost. Well let me tell you, you are not the only one.

When I think about that, I think of my friend, Maggie. Sitting down with her and hearing her story, you could see how her past was still affecting her and she was struggling to prevent it from spilling into her future. The biggest impact of her past wasn't even related to something she did. It was what *someone else* did.

Some battles can leave permanent scars, but Maggie is learning to get off the mat every day.

T: So what led you to the point where you wanted to take your own life?

M: I don't know. Depression is something that I have been struggling with—everyone in my family's dealt with it—and it's just like . . . I didn't care anymore. I looked at my dad and I was like, "If he could fight for so long and it still wasn't enough for him . . . like . . . why is it ever going to be enough for me?"

And that's one of the things I'm worried about most: that no matter how hard I try, that's in my DNA.

It's just like . . . give up. Just end it. And just stop trying.

"And that's one of the things I'm worried about most: that no matter how hard I try, that's in my DNA."

I am always on the lookout for hope. Hope, to me, is something that is rarely remembered but always needed. I will read books and watch movies all in the search for hope, but the best kind of hope is the kind that's displayed in real life. Such was the case for the Thai soccer team in 2018.

The Wild Boars soccer team and their coach entered caves in Northern Thailand for their traditional visit. It started to rain while they were down there, the water rising rapidly. Having trekked 2.5 miles into the caves, they were trapped on a small landing, water surrounding them. There was no food, no fresh water to drink, nothing. The only tool they had was rope, so the coach volunteered to tie it around himself, jump in, and see if he could swim to the other side.

It wasn't too long after that the boys had to pull him back to stop him from drowning. This team of twelve boys between the ages of eleven and sixteen were not only stuck but running out of air. As each day passed, they kept repeating the words Su-Su to each other. Keep fighting. Keep fighting. It was nine days before anyone discovered where the team was, and eight more days before each member was rescued safely.

It wasn't just the dripping water from a stalactite that helped them survive those seventeen days, but the mantra they kept repeating to each other:

Su-Su. Keep fighting.

Dealing with depression and having thoughts of making decisions with irreversible consequences is part of many people's journeys. To those who are personally struggling or know someone that is struggling, never stop repeating those words: Su-Su.

Keep fighting. Please. Keep fighting.

Don't give up on yourself. Don't give up on your friend. Holding onto hope for them is doing more than you know. If you feel pinned down on this part of your journey, Su-Su. Day after day. Even if fighting looks like taking a few baby steps forward, let that be a triumph. Raise your arm in victory to celebrate both the big and small wins.

And hold onto the hope that victory will come even if you feel pinned right now. The nine days with no promise of rescue were the days Su-Su was repeated most. Those were the days hope was held onto the tightest.

Day ten did arrive.

And so did day seventeen.

What's your definition of hope?

Scan the QR code to watch a message from
Terrence about reasons to

GET UP

When have YOU had to choose to
get up and keep fighting?
Write your story here:

Or draw it here:

Wreck this page!

Are you feeling stuck or pinned down at this point in your journey? Are you feeling let down or hurt, like you just can't catch a break? Maybe you've been holding it all in until this point. This is your space to let out your emotion. *Scribble, scratch, write in giant ALL CAPS letters—whatever you need to do! Let off some steam.*

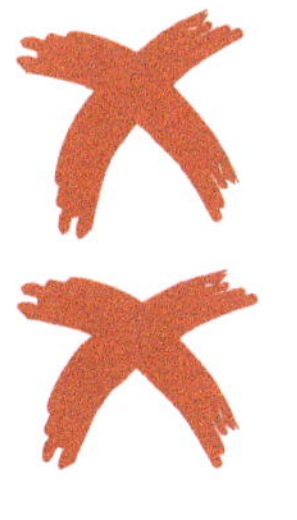

T: Has there been a way that you have chronicled your journey going forward?

M: Not really. It's kind of hard to think that I have a journey. 'Cause, this is just like, I am growing up knowing my dad died and that's normal for me. It's hard to think, "Oh, it's not normal for anyone else."

T: Maggie, you most certainly do have a journey! Your journey started when you were born and you grew up in such a hostile household and then at seven you had a traumatic event happen to you and then even now, dealing with the things that you're dealing with . . . I know that these are things that I dealt with. They're not something that you'll just be healed from and this will constantly be that darkness that you have to fight off. With that journey and where you're at right now, if you can go back, I know you're only fourteen years old, but if you can go back, is there a day that you remember with your dad that was a good day?

M: Yeah, he used to make nachos around Carsontmastime and he would put on this little elf hat. We would all sit around the fire and watch Carsontmas movies, and he would always move the chair up closer to the TV for me 'cause I was small and I wanted to see better.

Trust me: you're on a great journey too. And every great chronicled journey needs a title. Think of *The Fellowship of the Ring*, *Harry Potter and the Deathly Hallows*, and *The Hunger Games*. What's the name of your journey? (Don't just put "(Your Name)'s Journey." Get creative! As a matter of fact . . . draw the book cover for your story. I want to see something fantastical, wild, messy, and imperfect. It doesn't have to be perfect. It just has to be you.

What would you name your life journey so far?

Draw the cover for your life story here:

Drawing the Good Out of the Bad

T: Maggie, where did you get your passion for art?

M: Um . . . my dad loved to draw . . . that's one thing I remember about him. We would always sit down and color in coloring books together.

T: What?!

M: Yeah, he was a painter—he used to paint houses.

T: What?! Maggie, you didn't just inherit awful things, you inherited some great things about your dad, and obviously art is very healing for you.

Let Go

Draw a fire and write all of your negative thoughts about yourself or your situation in it. Feel free to rip this page out, crumple it up, tear it, and imagine those negative thoughts are being burned away.

RIP IT UP!

Rip this page up! Now, I didn't say rip it out. Rip this page as many times as you can without ripping it out of the book. I bet you can't make more than four big rips without taking the page out.

Seek Good.

Maggie inherited SO much more than a legacy of suicide from her father. She inherited a great sense of humor and love for art: two things that make up the core of who she is. I want you to take this away: you are more than your current circumstance. You are more than your past. You are your own. *Take some time to write out or draw the things that act as silver linings in your life. Maybe they're big or maybe they're small. Either way, I promise you they are meaningful.*

What's Your
SAFETY PLAN?

We can't be caught off guard. You know that moment when you feel good about the way things are going and the progress you're making, and you say to yourself, "I'm never going to let it get that bad again," or "As long as I don't have to deal with that situation or person, everything will be great"? But then something bad happens or someone new hurts you worse than before, and all of a sudden you're feeling like crap again.

I don't want that to happen to you. I want to help you sort through your issues (which I am not trained to do), but in order to do that, I'd have to invade your space and eat your cereal because sometimes it takes time—a lot of time—to sort through things.

Plus, I am an emotional guy, so there will be tears and snot. As you can imagine, it would become a whole thing. You don't want that. Trust me. That's why we need to make a plan before you find yourself in a bad situation. That way, when the time comes, you'll have things to help manage your emotions and navigate whatever situation you need to.

Warning Signs

List any thoughts, images, circumstances, or behaviors that indicate a crisis may be developing:

____

____

____

____

____

____

____

____

____

____

In Class Coping Strategies

What are some things you can do to steer your mind away from the problem and focus on what's in front of you? Maybe try a breathing exercise or focus on a particular object in the room.

1. _______________________________________

2. _______________________________________

3. _______________________________________

4. _______________________________________

Out of Class Coping Strategies

Think of some healthy strategies for addressing hardship when outside of school. Could you meditate, exercise, or talk with a loved one?

1. _______________________________________

2. _______________________________________

3. _______________________________________

4. _______________________________________

Internal/External Contacts

Make a list of people you can ask for help. They may be teachers, friends, counselors, or professional therapists/ clinicians.

1. Name____

Contact_____________________________________

2. Name____

Contact_____________________________________

3. Name____

Contact_____________________________________

4. Name____

Contact_____________________________________

5. Name____

Contact_____________________________________

6. Name____

Contact_____________________________________

Suicide Prevention Lifeline Phone: 1-800-273-TALK (8255)

So Here's the Plan

When having a difficult time, _________________ will first try an in class coping strategy. If this is insufficient, _________________ will notify the teacher and proceed to an out of class coping strategy. If the classroom teacher is in the middle of a lesson, _________________ will show the teacher their personal pass and proceed to the guidance office to speak to a trusted adult.

The one thing that is most important to me and worth living for is:

This is the page where you can take out all your frustrations. Scratch until it makes a hole in the page. Write what you wish you could say to someone or in this moment out loud. However you take out your frustrations, this is the page to do it on.

IF EVERYTHING WAS PERFECT, YOU WOULD NEVER LEARN AND YOU WOULD NEVER GROW.

Beyoncé

BE A HERO

The Importance of Showing Up for Others

It's amazing to see where Carson started and where he is now. There are so many shocking and inspirational moments in Carson's story, and I wouldn't be surprised if one day we're all reading his book. I heard Carson describe how, at an early age, he was caught in between two worlds. Not only did he feel that way because of the color of his skin, but he was also caught between being a straight-A student and a literal gang member. This constant struggle led him down a road that could have ended up very tragic for everyone around him. The start of his story is in that feeling of being lost, the feeling of trying to figure out where he's at.

I travel a lot for my job (when there is no global pandemic, at least). Sometimes I get to fly and be at my destination in a matter of a few hours, but there are times when I have to drive. Either my schedule is too crunched to find a flight, or it's just close enough that flying makes no sense. Whatever the reason is, I am forced to drive for long periods of time.

Anyway, when driving long ways, I always use my GPS on my phone to help keep me on the right track. But one day the map app got it wrong. I was driving in the dead of night in Iowa. By myself. It was raining, and there was nothing but cornfields around me (it was seriously a setup for a slasher movie). But I was driving on the highway, so it wasn't too bad. There were light posts every so often, and off-ramps were scattered along the road, so I could always pull off and stop somewhere if I had to.

The ride was taking forever though. I was exhausted from doing assemblies earlier that day, and I had more assemblies the next day. So of course, I needed to make this drive as short as possible. I pulled up my good old GPS and checked if there was a shorter way. And there it was, a route that cut out an hour and a half of my drive. All I needed to do was get off and take a few sideroads. No problem, right?

All of sudden, I was driving in between cornfields where there were no streetlights, and of course, the rain was getting worse. I realized at that point that I was driving on gravel. I looked, and my GPS still had me going down the "right" road and said I was only thirty minutes away. I looked around, and

there was a little town ahead. I pulled into it and noticed there were several abandoned houses around. I thought that was weird. I could see a church with its doors boarded up and a light up in the attic that was on. I was like, "Oh no, I am out!"

I drove fast to get out of that *Children of the Corn* creepy place, but then I suddenly had to stop. The road was closed ahead due to flooding. I whipped the car around and headed right back the way I came—got back on the highway having added two and half more hours onto the trip. I was upset but glad I didn't end up on *Unsolved Mysteries*.

You know what every mystery has in common on that show? Every mystery always starts with a person, alone, who disappears. Now, whenever I am afraid, if possible I always try to find someone else. When you're lost, it is so much harder to find your way when you're by yourself.

Everyone Needs Someone

When was a time you really could have used someone's help? Where were you? Write down a movie that would best describe that moment.

C: So all of this then leads to my story. I was born into an interracial marriage, in the 1970s in South Minneapolis, and I, for many, many years, once I got out of my childhood, didn't have an identity, to be honest with you. I wasn't black, I wasn't white. There wasn't really a clear category for what it meant to be biracial, because that was such a new thing, because it was illegal to marry interracially for so long.

Where is the start?

We all have to start somewhere. Something Carson said in his interview that stuck out to me when we first started talking was when I asked him to start at the beginning of his story. He said that he would start with his parents, because their stories are how his identity was formed. Too often, we start our stories with us, but our stories actually start with our parents' stories, or maybe even their parents or grandparents.

Write down your start. Where did your parent(s) start? Try to write a one sentence summary if you can. You can obviously write more than one, but keep it short. Feel free to draw it too!

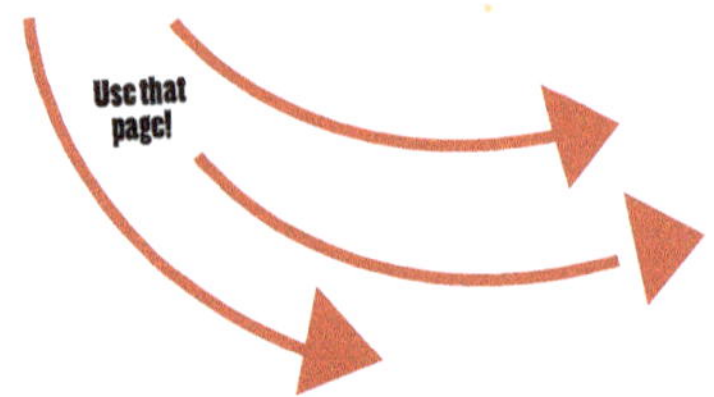

START

C: On the football field, I was a terror. I had this other life, because I was also an academic all-star. I was also a church boy, but that's a different story for a different day. In my other life, I was a monster. My job was to knock people out, so I perfected the one-punch knockout.

T: What did your parents do during that time? Did they see that change in you? How did they respond?

C: No, they didn't, and I don't blame them. I was just really really good at living multiple lives and hiding things. I was really smart, I had a 3.9 GPA, so I figured out who I needed to be when I was with my parents, and I was that person. I figured out who I needed to be at church, and I was that person. I figured out who I needed to be in the classroom, and I was that person. And I figured out who I needed to be on the streets, and I was that person. I mean, there were multiple versions of me walking around Minneapolis at that time.

"In my other life, I was a monster. My job was to knock people out…"

I need you to draw a picture of "perfect." What represents perfection to you? If you don't like drawing, cut out something that represents "perfect" and tape it on this page.

Then I want you to think of a secret. Hide your secret by writing one word that represents it somewhere within your picture. You think anybody can see it?

C: My senior year of high school, I ended up getting involved in a very serious crime. An armed robbery, where we almost killed a man in front of his child. I drove my parents' car to the crime scene in the middle of the night. I held the double-barrel shotgun. I was in the middle of the entire crime.

C: I was arrested on the football field, in my pads. Minneapolis high school football, playing in the championship.

T: Did you know this was coming down?

C: No, all of us who were involved in this basically scattered. We were laying low. But, you know, I was academic, so I had to show up to school and to football. So when I showed up and played in the football game, the police came to the game. I remember I was on the field, playing inside linebacker in the Twin Cities championship game. Coach called timeout, and there was a police officer standing next to him. And I was like, "Oh man, they got me."

Everyone Needs Help

On some of the biggest mountains in the world, people need an expert to be their guide. Most of the time, it's someone who lives around the area and knows the landscape pretty well. Even if you are an expert yourself, you still need that person to help get you started. It's really easy during times when we feel lonely, tired, or defeated that we forget about the people who have been there. We make excuses on why we can't reach out to them now.

"It's not that big of a deal. I don't need to call them."

"They're probably too busy for me."

Nope.

I am telling you they are not too busy for you. In fact, I can almost promise you they would love to hear from you.

Write down people who have made a difference in your life. How do they make you feel?

____

____

____

____

____

T: Was there anybody that you talked to throughout this process, or somebody that has been involved in your life journey? It is crazy how you went from almost going to prison for twenty years, and then now doing what you're doing – being active and having your doctorate. Is there anyone who walked with you through this whole process?

C: The person who has been most consistent and has been there at the key moments is a man by the name of Mike Johnson. He lives in Minneapolis, and when I was in high school, he was my youth pastor. So he had firsthand experience watching all of this. When I was locked up, he would come visit me. When I got out of trouble, he was there.

Mike Johnson is probably the most important man in my life. My dad is very important to me, and I love him, but Mike is probably the most important man in my life.

T: How did that bond form? What was it about Mike that made you trust him?

C: Well, I forgot to add one other thing Mike did. So, when I was in junior high and Mike was the youth leader at our church, my parents were done with me. Like, I was kinda being a knucklehead. It must have been eighth grade or ninth grade, I don't remember exactly when it was. They were like, "You gotta leave the house for a few days. We can't handle you here right now." So I moved into Mike's attic. Mike showed up. He's shown up for me every time I had a crisis.

Whenever we went to funerals when I was a kid (this makes it sound like we went to funerals every day, but I promise we didn't), my mom would always complain about how everyone spends money on flowers for someone who will never see them. To this day, she tells me to give her flowers now. She likes to look at them now. In her black mom voice, she says, "I don't care about them flowers when I am dead."

She's right. Why don't we give the roses to the people we care about now? We should let them know how we feel about them before a tragedy.

Write down the name of someone who has made a difference in your life. Then write how they've made that difference and how it made you feel. Then tear this page out and leave it somewhere you know they will find it. (Use the next page if you need to).

Carson and his mother

C: Life is a series of choices. Choose wisely. A single decision can change the trajectory of your life.

...

C: You're on the Earth for a reason, and whatever that reason is, we need you. We need you to show up. There are children who are being trafficked right now, waiting for you to show up. And if you don't show up, maybe no one will. There are kids stuck in horrific foster situations. Kids trapped down at the JDC, trying to figure out the future. These young people are waiting for you to show up. And maybe someone else will show up, maybe they won't. Maybe that's why you're here.

"Life is a series of choices. Choose wisely."

Scan the QR code to watch a message from Terrence about asking the question:

WHO IS YOUR HERO?

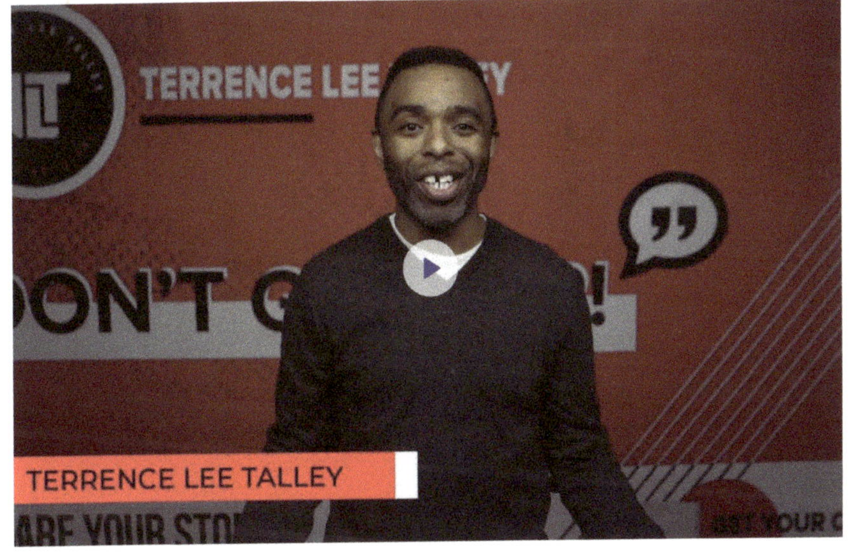

It's your time to show up.

There are people who are in need, and they are crying out that they need you. They need you when they turn down that scary road in the middle of Iowa. I know it may seem like you can't help people in a major way, but that's not true. I always felt like I couldn't make that difference. I wanted to, but I just couldn't. Until I focused on one person I wanted to help.

My brother.

My brother ended up taking his own life, and I wished I could have helped him more. Maybe I could have said more, done more. I started my first book, *Secrets Anonymous: OUR Story*, because I wanted to retroactively help him. His last words to me were, "Terrence, I love you. I am proud of you." He believed in me. I put on my cape for him, because he helped make it.

It's your turn to put your cape on so others will know they have one, too. ***Who are three people you can show up for, and how can you show up for them?***

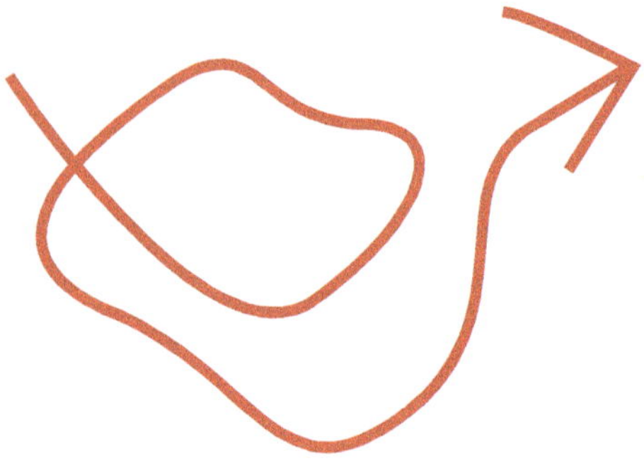

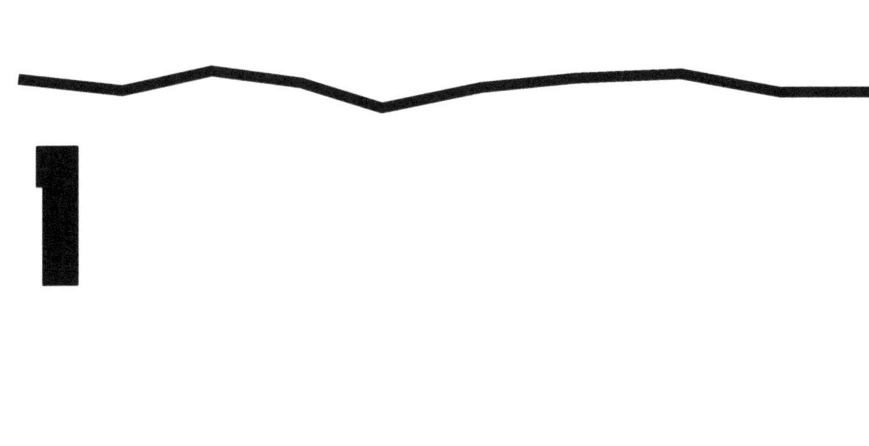

1
2

3

Draw the monster that you always imagined hiding underneath your bed when you were a kid. If you didn't have one, then make one up that would scare you now.

NO MATTER HOW YOU FEEL.

GET UP.

DRESS UP.

SHOW UP.

 AND NEVER

GIVE UP.

Daniel Craig

TAKE A REST
Rediscovering Your Self-Worth

Alex's life is a story of continually being treated like she's at the bottom. When you read this interview, think about how you would feel if you were in this situation and in what ways you can connect with her journey of being stuck on the bottom.

Have you ever wanted to throw a golf club? Every time I go mini-golfing, that's exactly what ends up happening. When I first start the game, I am super excited. I always think, *Here's my chance to be great at this ridiculous game and show everyone I can play with the best of them* (because no one goes mini-golfing alone). The first hole may go well, and I am running to get to the next one. The second hole— some stupid hill with uneven carpet—messes me up, so I get a point behind everyone. *I can still make a comeback though, right?* On the third hole, after the second time fishing my ball out the green-colored pond, a "friend" comes over and tries to give me advice, because apparently I look like I have no idea what I'm doing. *Shut up! Leave me alone. These people don't know me! They're just throwing off my concentration.*

Next thing I know, I am going to each hole saying that I hate this and am ready to leave. I look up and see everyone comparing scores and competing for the top spot. At this point, I am ready to break this club, throw the pieces to the eighteenth hole, and go to the café to eat popcorn by myself. I am exhausted by this whole experience and am convinced that I'm not good at anything. "You want to play again, Terrence?" *No, get out of my face. Mini golf is for people who hate their friends and love to see them suffer.*

But the problem isn't really mini golf, even though I hate that game. The problem is when I don't stop to take a

rest before spiraling down and getting used to being at the bottom. Some people and situations in your life might make you feel like you are always at the bottom of the heap. You get used to the shame, the defeat, and sometimes the abuse that comes with being at the bottom.

But you can stop it! Take a step back from all that and rest. See that your "mini golf" (your struggle) doesn't determine who you are.

When You Feel Less Than

*Write the things that make you feel worthless
on the lines below. On the next page, read
what I know is true about you.*

____

____

____

____

____

THAT'S NOT YOU

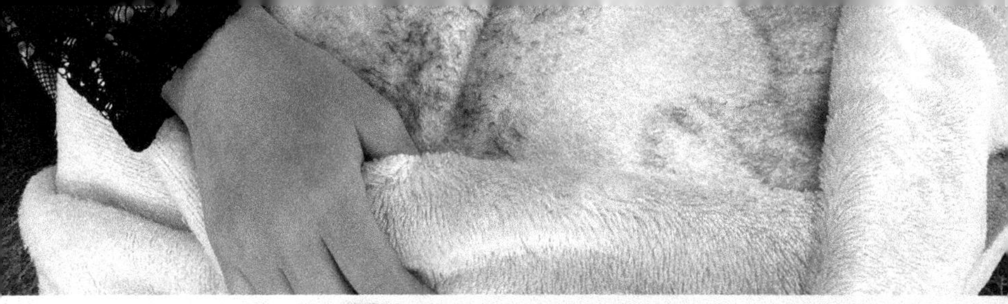

A: Most people find it pretty interesting that I'm nineteen and I've moved twenty times.

T: What?!

A: That's why I brought my baby blanket, actually. It's because that's the only thing that has been consistent. That's the only thing that I move from place to place with.

T: Well, tell me then, what was the first time you moved and why, if you can remember?

A: I do not remember. When I was a baby . . . I don't even count those moves. Like, I was born in Milwaukee, but that was just because they were passing through.

T: Well then, what was the first time that you remember, and why?

A: I remember moving from El Paso, Texas to Germany, and that was because my dad was in the military. He was in the Army, so we lived in a small town called Hanau for the first year and a half that we were there. And then that town got torn down. I was there for kindergarten.

T: What?!

A: Yeah, torn down. Like they took down the base. So we moved to Kaiserslautern, and I was supposed to . . . I was all registered to go to second grade there. And during the summer, my dad got deployed to Bulgaria. And I'm not allowed to legally live with my mom alone, so I got deployed to my aunt.

Getting Used to Garbage

The scariest TV show I've ever seen is the show *Hoarders*. If you haven't seen it, each episode follows two different people who struggle with hoarding objects (usually in their house). In the show, they have a counselor work with the hoarders to prepare them for the moment when it's time to clean up the house. It's important to clean the house, or else you're just living in the facade of change. Sometimes the people end up having to move anyway, but they've hopefully gone through the process of cleaning that first house so they can bring good habits to the next. When I watch that show, I always think, *How can they live like this?* But life is like that sometimes; your garbage builds up over time, and you get used to it. That becomes normal to you.

Sitting and talking with Alex about the part of her story when there was no stability, it was weird to hear her say that this was just normal to her. I get that sometimes our parents or life situations make it necessary for us to change where we live . . . but over *twenty times?!* Alex moved so much that she never had the opportunity to deal with some of the garbage that came up in the original house. You can and should, though.

Putting Garbage In Its Place

Label each garbage bag below with something that is weighing you down, causing you stress, or hurting you. Underneath, write out what you think is keeping you from throwing that garbage away.

T: Okay, that is a big part of this story. Why can't you live legally with your mom?

A: Most of it has to do with when I was younger. When I was two years old, all the pictures from when I was between two and four, my teeth are black and blue because she threw me into a wall in my highchair.

T: What?!

A: My aunt was saying something about how she's a terrible parent. And she was like, "Well if you want her, you can have her." And she just threw me in her direction, but not really at her, just into the wall.

T: As a baby, she did that to you?

A: Yeah, so in most of my baby pictures, my eyes are black and blue. My teeth are black and blue. And there was another time . . . I don't actually know if the cops got involved in that one. But I know there was another time in Texas when she dropped me off at a neighbor's house to hang out with friends, and she didn't come back for a week.

T: What?!

A: And then she called the cops saying that I was kidnapped. So then the neighbors told them what actually happened. So between that and a lot of other stuff in the past, they deemed her unstable. Like when my parents were dating, she told my dad that her brother was coming up with a Firebird from Florida. She did have a Firebird, I guess at one point, but not at that point. She also doesn't have a brother. So she gave the cops information about a stolen car. She gave them a fake social security number and a fake name for her fake brother. Sometimes she would have hour-long conversations with her other brother in prison. My mom has one sister.

Scan the QR code to watch a message from Terrence about

REST

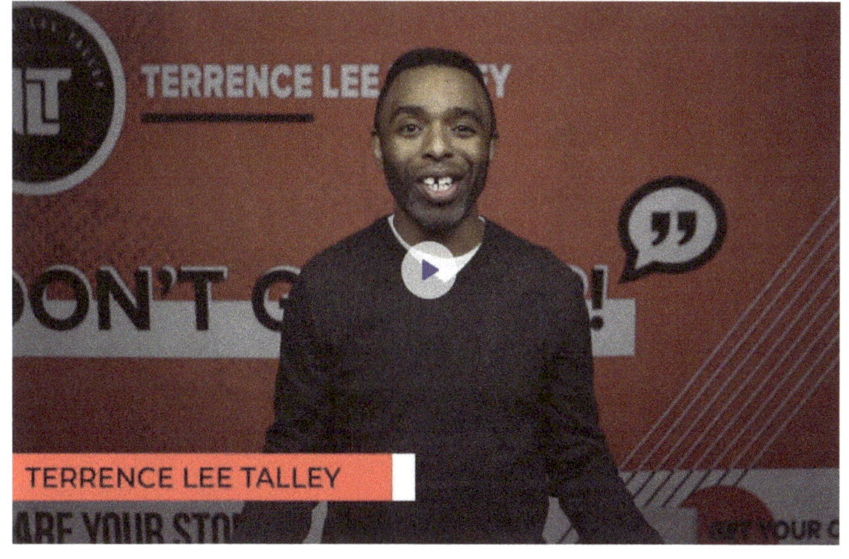

Coloring Outside the Lines

Coloring can be very traumatic for some of us. I'm serious. For me, coloring was the first time I felt I wasn't good enough. I remember sitting in kindergarten at this small kids' table, coloring some crazy drawing of a creepy little boy holding the letter T (see, it was so traumatic that I remember what the picture looked like). I was looking at all the other kids in my class who were coloring his socks a different color than his pants. They colored his hair within the lines that came from his head. It was ridiculous. These kids were like the children of Bob Ross (more on him later), whereas my boy had his shirt and hands the same color, with that color also spilling onto the T. For me, though, I thought it looked cool in a distinctly different kind of way. That's when my teacher looked over at me and said, "Try to stay within the lines."

You know what I say to that? NO! I don't have to stay within the lines. I like my messy-looking coloring skills. I don't know what or who made you think your "coloring" (or something about you) wasn't good enough, or that you weren't good enough, but you are enough to me.

You take this time and color however you want to, whatever you want to. If you don't like these coloring pages, then draw something on the back of them and color that! No second tries; the first try is great. All you perfectionists, I want you to color outside those lines. You don't have to be perfect for somebody to care about you. After that, take your colored picture and tape it on your fridge. It's good enough to be on mine, because it was made by you!

YOU ARE
WORTHY
of good things

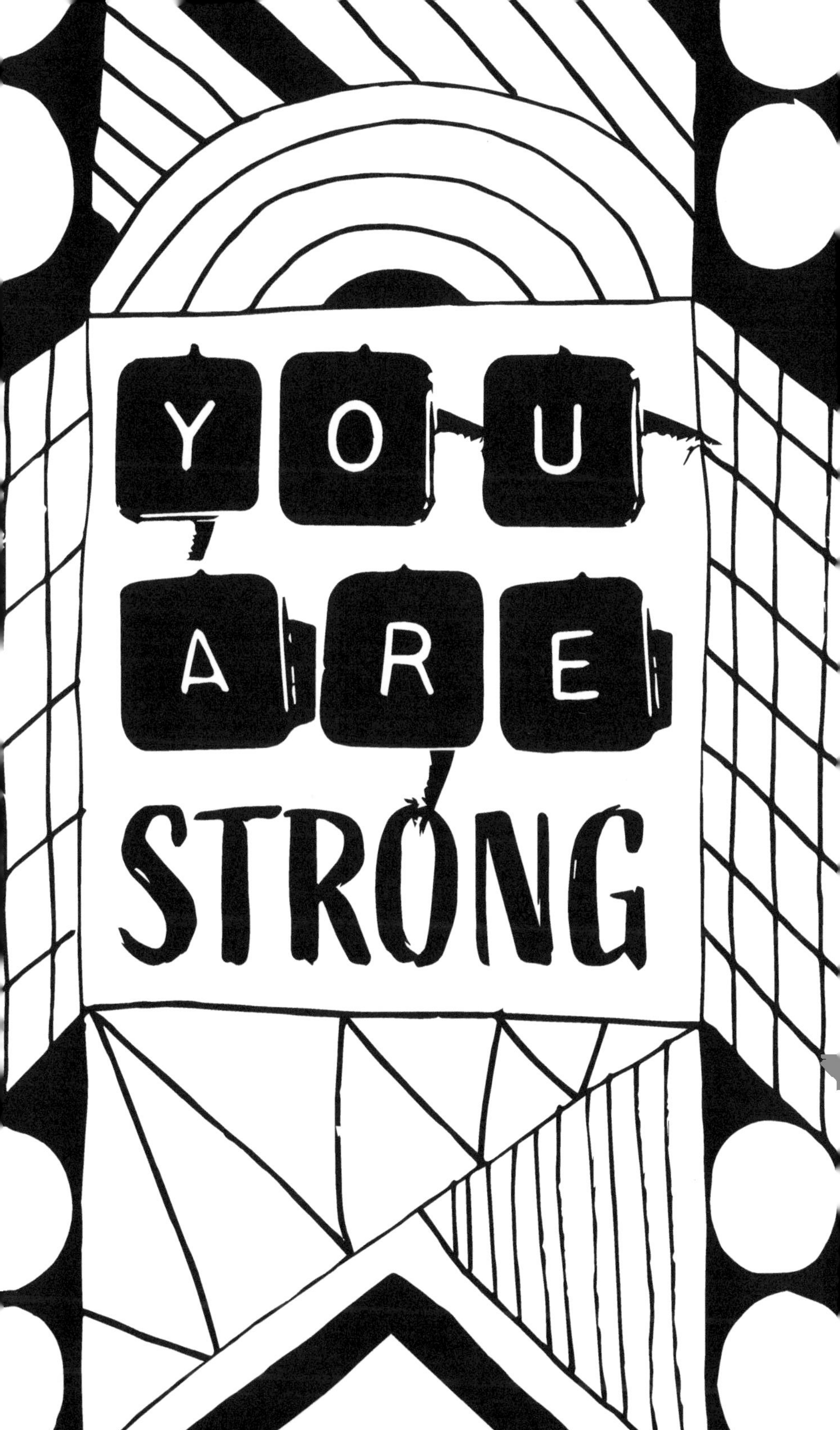

YOU
ARE
STRONG

YOU
ARE
ENOUGH

T: With your boyfriend, you said it was terrible. What made him terrible?

A: Well, we started dating in May of last year, and in April . . . No, we started dating in April, and then in May was prom. He didn't want me to go with friends or anything like that, so he went. I paid for his ticket.

T: Wait, how old is he?

A: He was a year older, so he had already graduated. It was my Senior prom. I didn't go to Junior prom, because I broke up with someone right before it, so I was like, "I don't really wanna go." He sat on his phone the entire time, did not get up once. I asked him to dance, he said no. He just kept asking me when we could leave. I was like, "I paid sixty dollars for your ticket."

T: Damn.

A: And I spent a lot of time crying. My friends were like, "Why are you with this guy?" I should've broken up with him that night, but he is so good at guilt-tripping, and making it, you know . . . He did feel bad, so he was crying, and I feel bad when people feel bad. So it's like, "Okay, we'll get through this." And it was that—all the time. You know, every time we went on a drive to Walmart or something, we'd end up crying, because he would say something that was just controlling, or . . . I don't know. I guess it really tipped over when I . . . I wrote a lot of poetry. I got a Gold Key award for the scholastic writing awards my senior year.

T: Yeah!

A: So I wrote him a song 'cause he liked my poetry. So, I wrote him a song for his birthday. And I showed it to a few of my friends, and they really loved it. And then I asked him if he wanted to hear it on his birthday, and he said no.

T: What, why?

A: Just didn't want to. And I was like, "I stayed up all night writing this."

T: So you're like, "Hey, I like you. I wrote a song for you." And he was like, "I don' t want to hear that."

A: Yep. And when my friend, Daren, said, "How did he react to the song?" and I said, "He didn't want to hear it," he was like, "What is wrong with this guy? Why are you with him?" And he just kept . . . I started talking to Daren more and more; I met him in one of my college classes. And the more that he heard about Mitch, the more he was like, you know, again, "Why?" And I did not want to be that girl that couldn't justify why I'm in a relationship like this.

T: Right.

A: So I told him I needed a break, because I wanted to keep trying to give it a chance, but I knew that Daren was a better friend to me than Mitch who was my boyfriend. And that's not right, because a boyfriend should be your best friend.

T: Right.

A: And then there was one night during that break that I was at the library at like ten o'clock at night – which you do when you're in college and studying – but he didn't believe me. And I kept telling him, "You need to calm down. I'm at the library." And he said, "Prove it." And I said, "I shouldn't have to. I've never done anything to lose your trust." But eventually I had to send him a picture of me in the library, and then he was fine. He was like, "I believe you." And I was like, "Yeah, well, *now* you believe me. You have to." After that, I was like, "This is not okay." So I moved out. Just moved into the dorm and put some stuff in storage units. My uncle owned storage units, so I could do that for free. And then I started dating Daren. My family loves him, which . . . they've never liked anyone. So it's a nice feeling.

We all go through hurt. For some, it's hurt from other people. For others, it's hurt from life situations that we feel broken down by. On the lines below, take the time to write down what's hurting you.

Now, read what you wrote. If you were talking to a friend who came to you with the same issues, what would you tell them? Below, write three things you would say to that friend.

This is what you need to say to yourself. Instead of blaming yourself or staying down, have compassion for yourself. Being a good friend to yourself is just as important as being a good friend to others.

Bob Ross is famous for Happy Trees (told you we'd get back to him). Maybe you've heard of Bob Ross, but he's the white guy with the big old afro who's always painting. He had a show of 400-plus episodes teaching millions of people how to paint. His goal for the show was to teach beginners how to paint. Tons of people watched, but not all of them watched to learn how to paint. A lot of people watched because Bob spoke so smoothly and peacefully in every episode. People felt comforted by him!

During the show, Bob would create original paintings right in front of your eyes, offering the viewer the opportunity to paint along with him. There were very few video edits throughout the whole run of the show, so you would see Bob mess up every once in awhile. He didn't get mad. He didn't throw the picture away. He would just stop for a second, look at the mistake, and then say, "What a great opportunity to make a happy tree." What's crazy is that he made it look like it was meant to be there. The paintings with those "Happy Trees" were still wanted by millions of people across the globe.

I am not telling you that abuse can be painted over. I am not telling you that all the things weighing you down can be turned into a "Happy Tree" moment. What I want you to know and see is that you are still valuable despite all of that weight and garbage. I may not have that same calming Bob Ross voice, but I want you to take a step back and rest in the fact that nothing will take your value away. I don't have a soothing voice, but I give comforting hugs. So picture that hug in your mind and let me assure you, your value isn't determined by your mistakes, how someone treats you, or your mini-golf score.

Rip this page out, and turn it into a bookmark for yourself. Write or draw something on it that would inspire you.

DON'T EVER
DOUBT
YOURSELVES
OR WASTE A
SECOND OF
YOUR LIFE.

IT'S TOO SHORT AND YOU'RE TOO SPECIAL.

Ariana Grande

TIME TO HEAL
Seeking Help with Self-Harm

I learned that my friend Darby has a lot of cuts. Interviewing her, I found myself constantly saying, "There can't be more, can there?" There were so many traumatic life events that she had to go through. The one question that kept coming up was: what did she do to get healthy? Even though you will only hear a part of her story, I think we can all learn from it.

Bandages

I have beef with bandages! You know, the sticky ones you put on cuts with a name we all use but I can't because of trademark rules. You know the ones I'm talking about. Starts with band and rhymes with paid. There are actually multiple different reasons why I am not a fan of any adhesive bandage. One: why do they never stick on for as long as you need them to? The only way to get them to stick is wrapping them around so tightly that you cut off all circulation—not to mention the whole water element. You get that bandage wet, and it's definitely coming off. Two: I hate all the different sizes. No matter what kind of cut you have, the bandage is either too small or big, too long or short. There is no in-between when it comes to trying to cover up a cut with these bandages. Three: how long does it need to stay on? Obviously, you want the wound to heal, but you don't want to leave it on so long that the bandage gets gross.

These are just a few of the reasons why I am not a sticky bandage guy. I didn't even bring up the icky residue afterward, the weird rubbery smell it has, or the mystery of antibiotic ointment (that's a weird word, but I guess it works).

If the cut always needs antibiotic, why not just make the bandage with it on there in the first place? The way I feel about cuts and bandages is how I feel when it comes to emotional cuts and time, too. Everyone always says, "Give it time," but time doesn't always seem like it does the trick. I always feel

like it's never enough time, or I've been giving it too much time. I don't know about you, but I've struggled with this my whole life.

How can I heal the emotional cuts?

In the space below, I want you to write words and phrases that represent a "cut" in your life. After that, put a bandage over each word or phrase. How many did you put on the page? Did they cover up the whole word/phrase?

T: And what was that last conversation like, with your dad? You said you were the last person to see him.

D: Correct, yeah.

T: What was that like?

D: You know, I go back to the day, and he . . . he didn't feel like himself. Like, I told him I loved him, and normally he'd say, "I love you, too." But, nothing from him. He seemed like he was . . . out of person. Like he was just not there.

T: Did he respond back to you or anything?

D: So that morning, me and my younger brother went to a gymnastics place for a little exercise, because me and him were both homeschooled. And my grandma couldn't find her keys, so she sent me back inside to go get them. And he was standing in the hallway, completely dressed, with the keys hanging off his finger. And I was in a rush, because I hate being late, but I said, "Bye! I love you, Papa!" And nothing. He just stood there.

I have a whole playlist dedicated to making myself feel better, songs that I connect with during difficult times in my life that help me in my healing process. I play the song "Praying" by Kesha when I feel like I am being told (or I am telling myself) that I am not good enough.

That feeling goes back to a time when I worked so hard to be in a school assembly organization. I had to submit video after video of myself speaking, because they kept on telling me I needed to add this, or say that line differently. After a couple of months and multiple videos, I got a call from the director of the organization flat-out telling me to stop sending stuff in because I "wasn't what they were looking for." They basically said I wasn't good enough, and it hurt. A lot. It made me feel worthless—but then I heard Kesha's song. Her song is about being taken advantage of and having her voice ignored (there's more to it than that, but I only have so much page here). It's also about Kesha standing up for herself and taking her power back. Obviously, her situation is a lot more serious than mine, but her song really encouraged me to get back up and let go of my anger. It helped me forgive myself and keep doing what I knew I could.

There is another song that has gotten me through a lot of hard times. "See You Again" by Wiz Khalifa always reminds me of my brother, Bug, who took his own life. That song helps me to remember the good times I had with him.

Listening to these songs has been a big part of my healing process. They have stopped me from living in my anger, and they bring me out of my sadness when I get stuck thinking about the things I've lost. They've stopped me from indulging in destructive behaviors when I am hurt. I think everybody should have a playlist like that.

Moving forward doesn't mean that you forget about what happened. I'll always remember my brother, but moving forward just means making the sting of the cut a little less painful. There are songs that can make you stay in your feelings and make you feel even sadder or angrier, but that is not what we're going for. Those songs don't help the healing process. Remember, we want to take time to heal.

*So what's on your playlist? Write down the titles
of the songs (and a lyric from each song) that
help you move forward.*

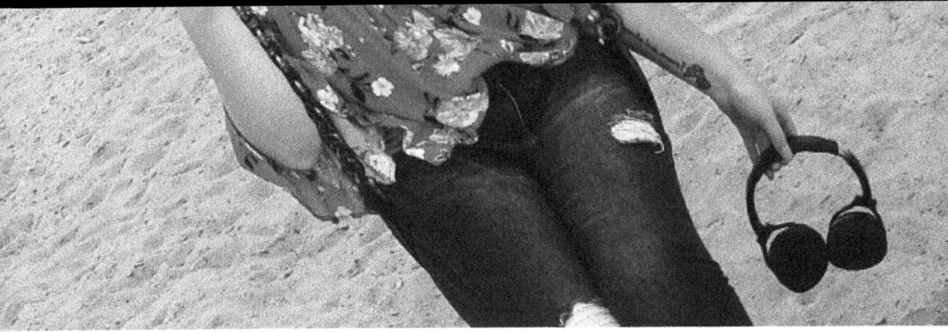

D: I did start spiraling. I had suicidal thoughts. I started cutting. So that was . . . the not-so-good part of that.

T: This might seem like a weird question, but do you have any close people—close friends—that just focus on you? Because it seems like, before you answer, it *seems* like since you have taken a lot of time to just take care of other people, have you really changed that about yourself? If that makes sense.

D: Yeah, absolutely. So I do have two, or three, really close friends that I absolutely adore. And they do so much for me. You know, just with my birthday passing, my friend was like, "I want to get you a birthday present!" And I was like, "You really don't have to," but she was like, "No, I'm getting you a present." No matter how much I feel like I don't deserve them, or like I'm bothering them, they always are like that. They say, "We love you no matter what. We're always gonna be there for you."

T: Do you sometimes feel like you're bothering people with your issues?

D: Absolutely, yes. It comes with the suicidal thoughts, but I do feel like I am bothering people . . . like my friends and family would be better off if I disappeared or died or whatever.

Scan the QR code to watch a message from Terrence about why it's

OKAY TO HEAL

My hope is that everyone has someone—that person you can go to when your life feels out of control and you don't know how to deal with the hurt. Unfortunately, I know sometimes that's not the case for a lot of people.

I talk to a lot of students after assemblies, and I can't tell you how many times I've heard, "I have no one." Maybe you have no one right now, but I believe everyone has possible allies around them, even if they just don't know it yet. *If you have someone that you can talk with who makes things easier or better, put their pictures or write their names on the next page as a reminder for when you have to let things out.*

If you can't think of someone, write down people you think might be good people to talk with in the space below. I challenge you to reach out to them and try to build that relationship (and I am not talking about a girlfriend or boyfriend relationship here; any bond can be its own type of relationship). I know it can be deathly scary for some, so I am not telling you to just pick someone real quick to get this done. Taking the time to heal means thinking through your steps of healing. So *take your time.*

Pictures Go Here

T: I know for me, one of the things that I wish was that somebody would have sat down with me and said, "Terrence, it's okay to ask for help. It's okay, I'm not going to judge you or think bad about you. You can ask for help from me, and I will give you help." What is it that you would want somebody to do for you?

D: Just to be there for me, to talk with me and say everything's gonna be okay.

T: Darby, everything is going to be okay. I am sorry for the things that have happened to you. You did not deserve any of those things, and you don't deserve the things that are happening to you right now. But, you are going to make it through this, and more than just get through this, you are going to thrive. And you said something that I think I would agree with. You are here, and there's a lot of people and students that . . . they're not here. They haven't made it, and they are struggling right now. What would you say to them?

D: It gets better, even if you feel like it doesn't. It does. You just have to wait for that light at the end of the tunnel.

The Truth About Bandages

Did you know that sticky bandages were invented by a guy whose wife was accident-prone? She kept accidentally cutting and burning herself, and each time he had to go into the room to help bandage the wound because his wife couldn't do it by herself. He invented sticky bandages because he didn't want to keep helping his wife. No matter what the package says, it can't help you heal faster. It's just there to stop the bleeding and prevent the open wound from getting infected. It can't fix the sting, fear, or embarrassment that comes from getting hurt. It can't substitute the healing touch of someone that says it's going to be okay.

My daughter, Cece, wants a bandage for everything. Fell on the ground, bandage. Somebody hit her, bandage. Her knee hurts, bandage. My wife and I were constantly buying bandages, because she was always trying to find a way to get them. Why though? Why does she want so many bandages, sometimes for wounds that you can't even see? It's simple, she wants us to focus on her when she's hurt, physically or emotionally. She falls off her bike, and even though it doesn't leave a mark, she wants the bandage because she is embarrassed. She wants to be reassured that we love her. She could probably do it herself, but she wants us to support her like a bandage can't.

That inventor might have had good intentions, but maybe his wife kind of enjoyed it when he paid attention to her hurt. The bandage is supposed to be used for the moment, but it doesn't take the place of actual healing. It doesn't heal deep wounds. We have to pay attention to our hurts and not only move on, but also try to heal ourselves. We have to stop sometimes and take a look at that wound. Sometimes you may need a professional to look at it, or you may need someone to put on some "ointment" to help it heal. All of this takes time.

You may say you disagree, but everyone loves it when other people show they care in loving ways. I am going to embarrass my little girls by hugging them and kissing them in front of their friends one day. Matter of fact, at eight and five years old, they have already experienced me kissing them and squeezing them in public. Every time they say, "Dad, you're embarrassing me," but they say it while laughing and smiling. They know their dad cares.

You deserve that. That's why you have to open up and let others in, so they can "embarrass" you too. A bandage just won't cut it.

It's simple. Make your best paper airplane with this page.

IF YOU'RE OFFERED A SEAT ON A ROCKET SHIP, DON'T ASK WHAT SEAT! JUST GET ON!

Sheryl Sandberg

FAMILY PROBLEMS

Lifting Yourself Up After Being Let Down

Dax's story is one I'll never forget. I met Dax during a youth outreach event where I was presenting. He told me one part of his story, and automatically I knew that I wanted his story in this journal. You are about to read only a short part of our interview together, but during all of it Dax was so happy. He lit up when we talked about all the people that helped him when he had nothing. I knew you should hear his story, because even in his worst moments of doubt and family drama, people showed they cared for Dax. And I promise you, there are people who care about you, too.

The Disney TV Family

I've figured out the Disney formula for their TV shows. First, it always has to take place in a unique type of location. Now this isn't for all of their shows, but it is for most. Maybe everyone is at Grandma's house, or it could take place at a summer camp that, for some reason, goes all year around, or it's possible that the family lives in a hotel. It sounds ridiculous, I know, but it's Disney. Next, there is always some weird family dynamic. On one show, the kids' parents are rich, and they leave them to live in an apartment by themselves. In another, the moms are best friends, and so both families share an apartment. There is even a show where everyone in the family is a spy. The final piece of a Disney show is that the kids are smarter than their parents, but the kids are always loved.

I don't know about you, but none of these shows are like my family. I once got a spanking for eating cold cereal on a Wednesday! Yeah, cereal. I want to see an episode where Raven does that to her kids. I always wanted my family to be one of those families, though.

My mom watched this show where the dad not only loved his kids no matter what, but he was also funny and taught them all valuable life lessons every episode. He even apologized to his kids if he made a mistake. My mom loved the show and so did I. I loved it so much that, now that I'm starting my own family, it's modeled on that. I do it because I loved how well the dad connected to his kids, even though there were times he didn't understand their perspectives. What show would you model your future family after, and why?

***What TV Family would you love to be part
of and why?***

____

____

____

____

____

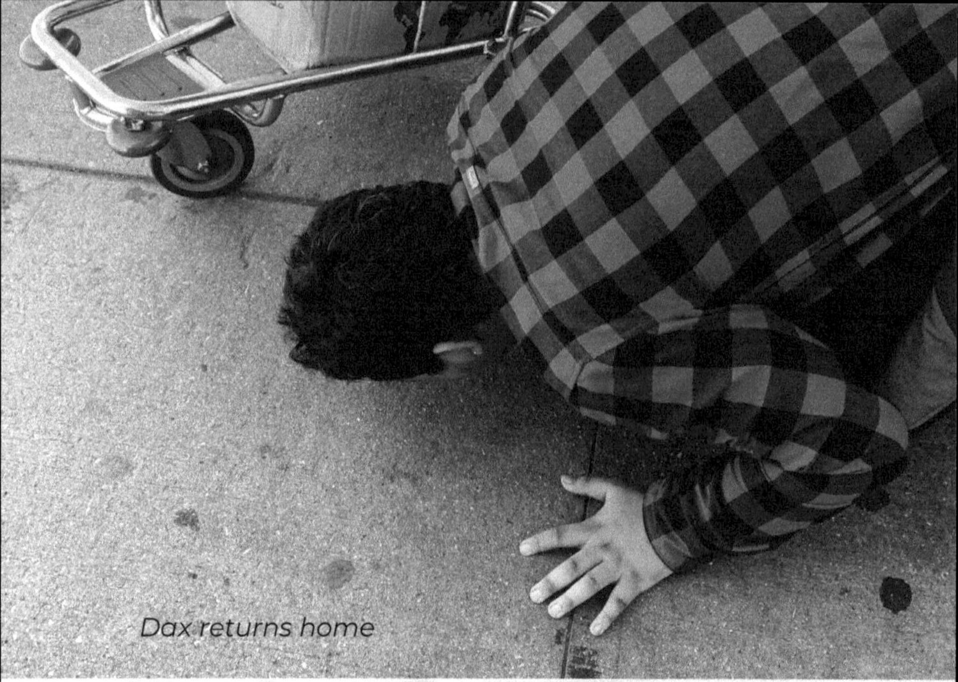

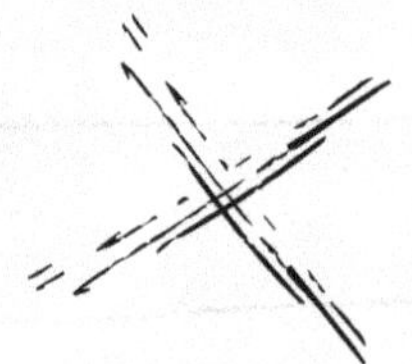

Dax returns home

T: You said that you were born in Nevada?

D: Yes, I was born in Las Vegas.

T: So, tell me a little bit about your story. Like, I know we talked a little bit about how you were born there, and then your mom left, or she didn't want to take care of you.

D: Okay so, of course, I was born in Las Vegas in March of 2002. Like, my mom had a family drama with my dad's family. And they kind of didn't work out. And pretty much, my mom . . . My dad didn't know what was gonna happen, but my mom was planning to bring me to the Philippines. Because, like, my dad is kind of full of . . . you know, false promises. He doesn't fulfill his promises. Like, he was supposed to get an apartment for my mom, but, you know, he's just all talk.

"...my dad is kind of full of...you know, false promises."

Have you ever seen someone sleeping in their car? Or seen someone asking strangers for money or food? You might think it would be really easy to spot, right? We have this picture in our heads of a car filled with stuff and a person sleeping right in the passenger seat—or someone holding a sign that literally says they need help—but it doesn't always look like that. There are people who need help, and sometimes we just have to look for them.

What would happen if we all took one day to search for one person in need? What is the extent that you could do to help them?

When you flip the page, you'll see a pair of eyes. *I want you to color the eyes in. Around them, write things that might be a sign that someone needs help. Then, write down five things you think you could do to help someone.* Not crazy unrealistic things, but something that is doable for you.

Next, tear that page out and put it in your pocket. That's right, put it in your pocket. If you don't have pockets, then put it somewhere you will touch it or see it often. Keep it there for one whole day. As you are going about your day, let it be a reminder to look for one person to reach out to. Just one. There are those like Dax out there who need someone to look for them so they can get the help they need. They need someone's help, and that someone is you.

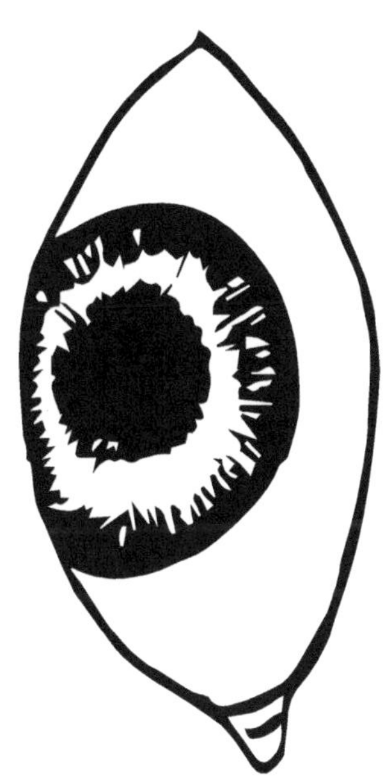

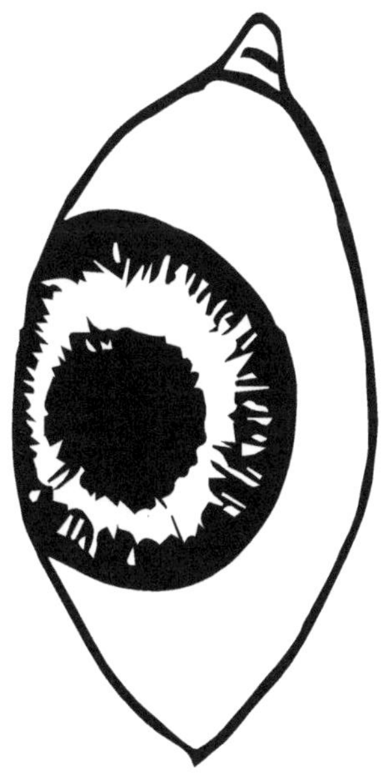

The Hard Truth

If you were open enough to give someone that page, you will see that they want to be there for you. If you couldn't, I want you to know I understand. The past might have shown you that people might let you down, they might lie to you. You know what? Sometimes they will; that's the hard truth. It doesn't mean they don't care, though.

You see, every year I take my two girls out on individual dates for Valentine's Day. My youngest daughter, Cece, couldn't care less about the date. One year, I bought Cece a new dress, took her to her favorite play place, and then we went to go get her favorite ice cream from Dairy Queen. I bought the cone and handed it to her. After the very first lick, she said, "Daddy, can we go home now? I want to be with Mommy." WHAT?! I made all these grand gestures and bought her all of her favorite things, but she still wanted to hang out with my wife more than me? Cece just does not care about Valentine's Day.

My oldest daughter, Gracie, is another matter. Throughout the whole year, she will tell me what she wants to do for Valentine's Day. She remembers what we did the year before and even has a paper ring countdown to Valentine's Day once February hits. She literally counts on me being there with her on Valentine's Day. And every year I tell her I am going to be there for her on Valentine's Day. Well, this past year that didn't happen, because I accidentally planned a school assembly tour that week. When I had to break the news to her, she had a total meltdown—we're talking tears and bubbles of snot coming out her nose. Then she said the line that we've all probably said to someone at some point: "You lied to me. You don't love me!"

I hated that. I didn't purposefully lie to her. I didn't try to let her down, but I did. One day, she's going to find this journal and write down ways I let her down. I love her with all my heart, but I have let her down. I hope she gives me grace and still knows I am someone that wants to pick her back up (even when I am the one who let her down). I don't know everyone's situation, but I do know there are probably people you're thinking of that are like me. I want you to know that I love you, and you can still trust people. You don't have to trust everyone. I would actually advise against that, but I know that the people who wrote (or would have written) on your page truly want to help pick you up. They just need you to give them a chance, even when they are not perfect at it.

T: This is a lot. Once you get to the Philippines, your mom leaves you with your grandmother, but then she has to work. From then on, you're bounced around to different family members for several years. So basically, your developmental years you're left to figure things out on your own with little emotional connection. Everybody has a way to deal with pain and hurt. If they're not talking it out, there's something that they do. What is it that you do to deal with all this?

D: You know, I just go with the flow . . .

T: You know, I hear ya, but there's got to be something that you—whether it's healthy or unhealthy—a way that you're dealing with all of this.

D: Yeah. So, I just . . . pretty much, I don't . . . like, the people that I'm living with in Las Vegas are not productive with, you know, that. So I just go put my headphones on, play video games, and forget about it.

T: I want you to be free with whatever you want to say, and I assure you number one: I'm the last person to judge anybody, so there's no judgement coming from me. I wanna assure you that those same emotions, and that same abandonment, there are students that are dealing with that even right now. And so, what is it—and once again, you can tell me you do nothing with it and you're just quiet and go along with everything—but, is there some way that you deal with this? Like, for some people, they'll go towards drugs and alcohol. Other people, they might go to pornography. Is there something that you do that you're like, "This is what I do to deal"?

D: Yeah, so, my dad lets me drink. So, you know, yeah I drank before . . .

T: Really?

D: Yeah, like, I just smoked cigarettes before, and stuff.

T: And is this still something you use to deal with things?

D: Pretty much I just drink now, so . . . not smoking. Smoking kills.

T: Yes, yes it does.

How Do You Deal With Those Rocks?

Dax has had to deal with a lot. I knew while talking with him that there was something he must be doing to cope with it. I had to poke him, but he eventually let it out. From there, we talked about a good way to relieve the burden he's carrying. It may involve a guitar and a song about a girl who put him into the friend-zone, but you'd have to ask him yourself about that.

On the rocks below, write down all the bad ways you deal with drama, being let down, and all the other things that drop a heavy weight on your life. Then pick one of those rocks and scratch it out until you can't even see it anymore. Next to it, write as "loud" as you can: "I HATE THAT! I AM NOT DOING THAT ANYMORE!" We can't be perfect, but we can work on one thing at a time. Once you know you are fully done and have no urge to do that one thing anymore, pick another rock and cross the heck out of that one, too. One day you will see, you don't need to keep carrying those stupid rocks anymore.

THERE'S SOMEONE WHO
WANTS TO HELP YOU

D: So, on July 31st when I moved back to the area, I met Tommy. I had dinner with my uncle, and he offered me a place to stay. I didn't stay because I really wanted to have pride with myself. Like, I didn't want him to step on me. So I left and Tommy's friend booked me a hotel, just for the night, and I met Tommy Saturday morning. And . . . yeah. We talked and we talked. And I'd gone to a few churches, asking for help, but none of them were available, and that night I slept at the Campus Life Center. By Sunday... I almost slept in my car. A friend called and he said, "Wait for me for an hour. There's a family that would like to help you." I stayed with the family for a week... Yeah, and this family helped me get housing. They got me connected with a case worker. I stayed in a hotel again for a week and then stayed in a boy's group home. It's kinda . . . kinda like an orphanage. And August 28th, I got my place, my apartment.

Scan the QR code to watch a message from Terrence about

BEING IN THIS TOGETHER

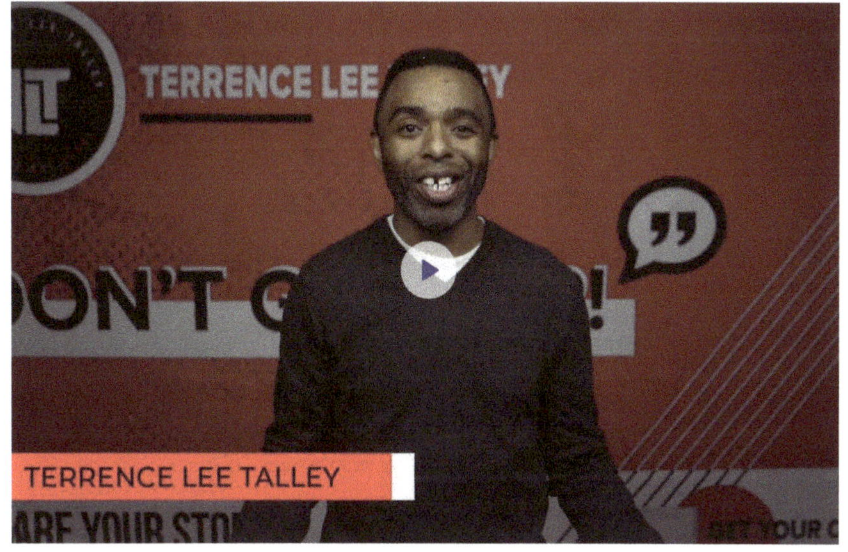

We all want someone to be there for us, even if you say you don't. You want people there for you, too. That's why we have to be there for others. In each of the four squares below, I want you to write someone's name in the middle of the square. Then, below or around their name, I want you to write how you are going to support them going forward. Once you do that, tear it out and give it to that person. They might not show it at first, but it's going to mean something to them.

I don't care what kind of music fan you are, you have to love a good bonding song. Before Eminem was considered one of the greatest emcees of all time, he was Marshall Mathers: a white, ninth-grade dropout who was homeless at twenty-five with a two-year-old daughter and girlfriend who was in need of help. He wanted to make a career in hip-hop, and it wasn't working out. He made music, had been on local radio shows, and won some rap battles, but it wasn't paying the bills. With his last remaining dollars and a final push to see what he could do, he went to LA to compete in the worldwide rap-battle Olympics. He was great, but he still didn't win. He left LA, calling it quits on himself and his dreams.

Enter Dr. Dre, a famous record producer. Now, I don't have the page-length or the time to fully explain who he is, so to sum him up, Dr. Dre was one of the biggest hip-hop producers in the game and has sold countless records. Dre was looking to restart his career, but he needed a new artist. After being handed a cassette tape (look it up) of Eminem's, he listened to it and knew he wanted to work with this guy. When he told the record label this was his guy, they laughed at him. Who wants to see a blond, little white dude rap? Dre pitched in all the money he could pull together and told the record company that if Eminem didn't work out, they could take it all and he would be done with his career. They never got the money that was on that table.

I watched a documentary on Dr. Dre and Eminem, and it was awesome hearing them tell the story from their separate perspectives. Each one told a different account of the story. Each one emphasized different parts of their relationship. They even admired different things about each other. At the end of the documentary, though, they both said the same thing. When asked about one another in separate interviews, they both said, "I wouldn't have made it without him. We got through it together."

You are going to make it past all this drama. There are people you may not even know of yet that are rooting you on. Throughout this section, you were asked to do something for someone else and read someone else's thoughts. Why? So you can see that you're not in this alone. We're in this together. It has been said that, "If you want to go fast, go alone. If you want to go far, go together." This life is a marathon; that's why you have to open up. Let someone in on your marathon so that when you start falling behind, they can help pull you up.

You got this! We got this!

Have you ever wondered what you would look like as a stick person? Not every person can draw well, but everyone can make a stick person. Draw yourself as a stick person. After that, draw your friends as stick people, too. It's weird, but aren't we all a little weird?

DON'T FEEL
STUPID
IF YOU
DON'T LIKE
WHAT
EVERYONE
ELSE
PRETENDS

TO LOVE.

Emma Watson

CELEBRATING YOU

Loving Yourself and Overcoming Anxiety

Riley was a straight-A student who dreamed of going to college and having a great future ahead of her. Meeting one person could change all of that. She went from being confident to doubting if she was valuable at all.

It might be hard to imagine, but that revelation can come so fast that it catches you off guard. A devastating journey through an abusive relationship and wanting to give up on herself, this is Riley's story.

I always admired the famous Mattel doll. Yeah, that's right, I am talking about the Barbie® doll. Over the course of sixty+ years, this character has held countless jobs, bought a number of different houses and cars, won beauty pageants, maintained a wardrobe second to none, and always looked like she doesn't have a care in the world.

But how? I know that isn't my life. My daughter, Cece, has started playing with Barbie® dolls (By the time you read this, who knows what she'll be into next...), and she loves the idea of playing with this doll that has "perfect" hair and can do anything she can think of. That's a great message for her to learn, but I just don't think this doll portrays a realistic view of it. I want to see *that* Barbie® doll – a realistic one.

I want my Cece to see the doll who is a firefighter, who has dirty hands and black smoke on her face from fighting a fire. I want her to have a Barbie® doll who is a doctor with bags underneath her eyes and streaks of grey in her hair, because she's been doing an all-night shift and is tired, but she loves her job anyway. I want Cece to have a doll that has endured stress and anxiety but is making it through.

Where is that Barbie® doll? I know Cece is going to endure all these things, and I don't want her to compare herself to "perfect." I don't want her to compare herself to anybody.

There are a number of things that can cause stress, and there is no need to add more stress because you think someone else is managing it better than you.

We Shall Overcome

Write down the things on the wave that you find overwhelming. Like a wave, things WILL subside and become less overwhelming.

T: Did you know that you needed to go to counseling?

R: Yeah, I think so. I started out doing some phone counseling here and there. I've probably seen, I wanna say, between maybe five and seven different therapists over the years. And the amount of time I've spent total is probably at least five to seven years of counseling. So I've gone through a lot.

T: Well, number one, why did you go through so many counselors?

R: I think it was just different time points. You know, I felt like, so maybe I do . . . like, I remember one that I had, she retired. I was maybe two years in with her, and I thought, "I think I'll be okay for a while." But then something else would happen and bring something else up. And then I'd have to find somebody else.

T: So what was it then? Because obviously you were starting to notice something in you that you were not okay with. But what was that?

R: I have a lot of anxiety. Almost panic attacks, sometimes, and I didn't realize what they were, at first. I think I remember sitting at the computer one day, and I was like, "Why does it feel like I have really bad heartburn?" But it was a really bad anxiety attack that was . . . I don't know. It was weird, first recognizing those symptoms of anxiety. And then I had no self-worth. I knew I had no self-worth. I think I was just really . . . lost, as to where to go next. And I knew by the time I left my marriage that I was dealing with a lot of abuse. I knew what it was, and I was telling people what was going on, but they didn't want to believe me.

Stop Talking, Carl

Have you ever fought yourself in your head? There's that moment when you're starting to feel good about something, but then someone says something, or you think something negative, and then doubt starts to creep in. *Was that person just saying that to get me to leave them alone? That repsonse was good . . . right? Things aren't going to be okay, are they*?

I hate that voice. For Riley, it was a real person. But for me, it's that person inside my head. I *want* to think good things. I *want* to be optimistic, but that *voice*! Why is it so loud? That's not the Terrence I want to be, so I've decided that's not me. It's Carl. I don't like Carl (to all you Carls in the world, I am sorry, but the voice just sounds like a Carl to me). If I can separate him from myself, it makes it a lot easier to silence him.

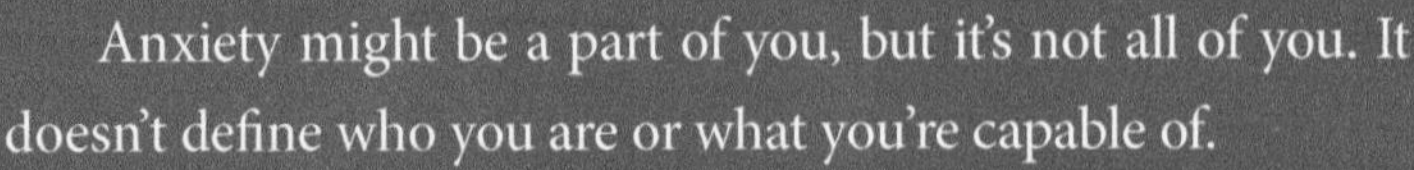

Where Is the Start?

Anxiety might be a part of you, but it's not all of you. It doesn't define who you are or what you're capable of.

Give a name to your anxiety. It might sound crazy, but giving it a name helps you establish a degree of separation between you and the anxiety. Amy, Barb, Duke, whatever! Let it present an opportunity to look anxiety in the face and say, "I hear you, _________________. I know you're just trying to warn me and protect me from bad situations, but I don't need you right now. I'm breathing. I'm whole. I'm okay."

T: So, because in my mind ... there probably is some girl out there that is thirteen years old, and she is that grade-A student, and it's like . . . How do you get from thirteen, a straight-A student, to twenty-four and just not feeling like that? Not feeling tenacious no more, not feeling confident in who you are. What would you say to that thirteen year-old who feels like that can't happen?

R: That's a really good question . . . It comes down to being really careful about the people you allow in your life. You know, as far as people that you're dating or who you decide to marry. And making sure that you have your own belief in yourself and your own confidence. It's going to keep you from looking for validation in other people.

144

Netflix has way too many TV shows. Matter of fact, it offers more than 1,300 shows. But within that amount of TV shows, there is a small amount of reality TV shows (smaller than what you would think, at least).

My favorite out of all of them is a show called *The Circle*, a gameshow designed around social media. The premise is, there are ten people living in an apartment building together, and they communicate by using a social media app (*The Circle*) designed for the show. Every episode, the contestants rank each other based on how much they like everyone. The catch: they never see each other or hear each other's voices. Their only communication is through their social media account. They don't know who's catfishing each other, and they don't know what people are saying behind each other's backs. They compete in random social media games, and then the contestants rank everyone. The two people with the highest scores get to become the "Influencers." In a private digital chat, those two people pick who is getting kicked out.

It's crazy! In every episode, they watch their screens to see what their score is and who's getting kicked out. My favorite character on the show is Carson. Carson has me cracking up every single episode. Before the revealing part of the episode, he always gets super dressed up, grabs his drink, treats himself to a nice dinner, and has fun with it. Of course, he's nervous that he is going to kicked off, but at the same time, he's constantly telling himself and yelling at the screen that he's beautiful. He came on the show to win, obviously, but at the end of the day, he's not letting this game tell him how beautiful and great he is. He's not cocky, but he knows his worth and that he deserves to be celebrated despite the outcome of the night. I love Carson! His confidence is what I want to have. I think we all should have confidence like that.

The first step to self-confidence is knowing that you deserve to be celebrated. It doesn't mean you're perfect, it just means you're proud of who you are and the work you put in. Celebrate it. Treat yo' self!

Celebrate It

In the boxes below, put something about yourself that you would like to celebrate. And then, in the box across from it, write how you are going to do that. As much as I would love to celebrate myself with a Lambeau Leap after putting this journal together, it's definitely not going to happen. I can celebrate, though, with a steak. Make it realistic so you can really celebrate you.

T: So let's go—we're going back to fourteen-year-old Riley. What would you say, knowing everything you know now about what's going to happen? What would you say to Riley, and obviously, you can't be like, "Don't marry this guy!"

R: I think it goes back to knowing your own value and self-worth. Believing that you have a lot to offer the world. Pursuing your own dreams first, before anyone else's. Knowing what you will and will not tolerate, and making sure you stick by that. It's hard to imagine me having that, because it wasn't instilled in me as a kid, by my parents. So what do you do for a kid that can't get it from their parents? I don't know.

T: Right. If you had a choice, are you proud to say . . . Would you want your girls to look at you, right now, would you be proud for them to see who you are right now?

R: Yeah, absolutely. We just bought a house in 2018, so I've been working a long time towards that. I bought it myself. There is nobody else on that mortgage. It's just me. I've worked hard to get where I'm at now. I wanna take nice vacations, when we can, when there's no pandemic. We can do fun stuff together. We have fun things we enjoy doing. My older daughter and I go skiing together. My younger daughter and I, well, she likes to bake. So things like that. We have passions that we are involved with.

Scan the QR code to watch a message from
Terrence about why to

TREAT YO SELF

TERRENCE LEE TALLEY

DON'T G

TERRENCE LEE TALLEY

ARE YOUR STO

You heard what I said. Treat yo self! Because you *are* worthy of good things. Maybe treating yourself looks like getting something from your favorite bakery or custard shoppe. Maybe it looks like taking a day or evening to unwind and take a break from everything. Here's the great thing: treating yourself is about taking care of *you* and *your* needs. It's about celebrating you and how strong you are and how great you are! ***My challenge to you is to treat yourself this week. Make a list of ways you can do that!***

-

-

-

-

-

-

-

-

Play Well

I thought about Riley's question a lot. How do you give someone confidence if they don't get it from their parents? How do you silence Carl's voice when he starts speaking anxiety in you? You have to build self-worth. You have to create steps.

That's where LEGO® bricks come in. The man who created LEGO® bricks is (he's Danish, hence Ole). He started off as a carpenter, making ladders and furniture in his own shop in 1916. Things went well, but one day his sons accidentally burned down the shop right before he was going to expand his business. Despite the major setback, he used it as motivation to build bigger and better.

But then the stock market crashed. Then his wife died. Then he became bankrupt.

So in the midst of trying to sell off the little he had left, he created inexpensive things to make ends meet. Amongst those inexpensive things was a toy. It didn't work at first, but he got a loan, and he loved the toy so much that it pushed him forward. He even named the company after this toy. That toy was what we now know as LEGO® bricks. In Danish, it means: "Play Well." There is a lot more to the story, and two more fires happened, but he plowed through. Despite all the bad, uncontrollable things that happened, Ole Kirk Carsontiansen built something bigger and better each time.

Was he all smiles every time he failed? Nope. He wanted to give up numerous times. But, just like the little blocks he built, his confidence was built a little bigger. If you want more confidence, participate in things that help build it up. You need to have confidence in *yourself,* not your *skill level.* If you want to fight anxiety, create steps to overcome it. Anxiety is more than likely going to continue being a part of your life, so plan on it. Take steps to seek help and fight it back a little more each time.

I am glad Cece likes playing with LEGO® bricks, too. When you play with creative, inspiring toys like that, you are truly playing well.

What did you want to be when you were a kid?
Draw it on this page. Let's see what you dreamed.

FAILURE IS
A GREAT
TEACHER AND,
IF YOU ARE
OPEN TO IT,
EVERY
MISTAKE HAS
A LESSON

TO OFFER.

Oprah Winfrey

LIFE CHANGES

Asking for Help and Healing from Addiction

*Things can change in an instant. There are
things that can alter our lives like the pandemic did,
but sometimes things can change dramatically by the
choices we make. Even the response to iceberg-level
events in our lives can alter our direction. Sarah
knows this all too well. My hope is that everyone
who reads her story will not only have empathy
for those caught in addiction, but also let those
struggling with addiction know that they are not
alone. Your iceberg is not the end of your story, just
the next part that has to be overcome.*

Iceberg Right Ahead!

In 1997, a little movie called *Titanic* came out (see what I did there?). It's about this kid named Jack who is this poor artist who luckily finds his way onto the Titanic. Meanwhile, Rose, a seventeen-year-old well-off girl, is brought onto the Titanic by her rich, stuck-up (there are so many things I want to call him, but I'll let your imagination fill it in) fiancé Cal. Rose is feeling trapped in this relationship and in her "high-class" life and decides she wants to end it by jumping off the ship into the freezing cold water of the North Atlantic Ocean (think Greenland). Right before she jumps, Jack comes along and talks her down. At this point, you're watching their love story unfold. Jack opens her eyes to a fun, exciting world, she tells him she's flying, blah blah blah. Typical love story stuff, right? Then next thing you know, the ship's captain notices that the Titanic is on a collision course with an iceberg and there is no time left to move the ship out of the way. BOOM! They hit it, and the second half of the movie begins. The story is not the story Jack and Rose were expecting.

Okay, let's talk about the elephant in the room. Depending on when you're reading this, we are either in a global pandemic or just getting out of one. No matter where you are at, this event has changed everything. We were not ready for this. Schools halted, jobs were lost, and life seemed to instantly stop for some. My job as a school assembly speaker, done. For Jack and Rose, they were scared when the iceberg hit. When the pandemic happened, some were scared as well, but for me, I was angry!

Here are some scattered feeling words. Stab a hole with your pencil on the words that relate to you for when the pandemic happened, or even for right now. Then proceed to write down why you chose that word on the next page.

Troubled
Withdrawn
Depressed
Overloaded
Empathetic
Jumpy
Spiteful
Wishful
Alarmed
Outraged
Hesitant
Needy
Competent
Naive
Brave
Worthless
Afraid
Neglected
Abandoned
Curious
Caring
Compassionate
Serious
Confused
Anxious
Bewildered
Invisible
Lonely

The Why

Scan the QR code to watch a message
from Terrence about

WHEN CHANGE COMES

S: I was a varsity cross-country runner. I was good at what I did. But after a while with being with that crowd, I, ya know, was doing well still until my parents got divorced. They got divorced and didn't tell me. I found the divorce papers, and I promptly ran away.

T: Wait a minute, like, just one day, they're like, "Yeah we're divorced."

S: I found the papers, and they didn't even tell me. They had been divorced for about eight months when I ran across the divorce papers. Mind you, I was like fourteen, fifteen years old and felt old enough to know this information, and I wasn't apparently. And so they broke my trust with that. I felt deceived. And then I moved to Burnsville, and I did not feel like I fit in anywhere, really. So it was a really tough transition for me.

T: Why didn't you feel like you fit in?

S: I am not sure, really. I think I had very low self-esteem. I felt that I was hideous-looking and poor and my clothes were... I was wearing my Dad's fishing shirts to school because my parents couldn't afford to get me nice stuff. And it wasn't about me wanting expensive stuff, but it was about me wanting to fit in. And I didn't feel like I fit in, but I also didn't want to ask my parents for stuff that I knew they couldn't afford.

Listening to how Sarah felt like she didn't fit in reminded me of writing. I am not going to lie, I wasn't a good student in my writing class senior year. My girlfriend and a number of my friends were in the class with me. I felt bad for my teacher, Mrs. Wells. I had to impress my girlfriend, and I had to entertain my friends. What was I supposed to do besides cause trouble? (If you are a student, DO NOT DO THAT. I don't need more writing teachers from across the country coming after me.) One day, we were given the assignment to write a poem. To be funny, I wrote... an obscene poem. I wasn't going to read it out loud in class, it was just for my friends and me. When Mrs. Wells asked for volunteers to read their poems, somebody dared me to read mine. What was I supposed to do? I couldn't say no. (YES, you can. Always say no in situations like this.) So, of course, I raised my hand. I didn't even get to the second line of the poem when I was thrown out of the class and sent to the office. Everyone ended up laughing except my best friend. I came to find out he had written this poem that revealed a lot about who he was and struck a chord with a lot of people in the class. His poem ended up being in our senior writing book while I was nearly expelled from school for the second time that year (the first time I almost got expelled is another story) and had to write an apology letter to read out loud to the whole class before I was accepted back into school. I always wondered what would have happened if I had taken that assignment seriously. Maybe someone would have recognized that I was struggling with liking myself, like they were. Maybe there was another like me who felt like they didn't fit in. Maybe a Sarah wouldn't have felt so alone.

Haiku for You!

We are going to write some poems. There are some of you that have been writing poems since you could crawl, and I am sure there are others like myself that are thinking they can't write anything creatively. The best part about creative writing is that it's an art: maybe there's no right or wrong, just be sure that it's true to you. So, we are going to write short haikus in the lines below. They're pretty easy. Plus, it's a great way to get some of those feelings out about big iceberg moments in your life. The first line is five syllables, second line is seven, and then end on the third line with another five syllables. Don't feel embarrassed if you don't know or remember what a syllable is. I had to look it up.

Write your haikus below!

S: Crestwood Alternative, it's a drug haven. So when I got there, it's like, there was a wider array of drugs available. Easily. Just go to school, there it is.

T: Did you feel more comfortable with those students there since they were the rejected, like the students that were pushed off to the side?

S: Yeah. And that's where I met my kid's dad.

. . .

S: I got to Crestwood, and I drowned that pain in heavy drugs. I wasn't just smoking weed and drinking with my friends.

T: Now, when you say heavy drugs, what do you mean? I want you to picture what these students are going through like what you're going through. Like, what do you mean by "heavy drugs"?

S: Well, I went to cocaine, then it was meth, and then it was crack. Literally, by the time I was sixteen, I was driving my car into the ghetto of Minneapolis. By myself, in the middle of the night. Letting weird, random drug dealer dudes in my car to sell me crack.

Where Is It At?

Now, to get the help we need or to help someone who is caught in a situation where they may need outside help, we have to know where to go. I can't tell you how many times I've heard students say that they need help but do not know where to go or who to talk to. I promise, there are places where you can go to get help. Trust me on that. So now we have to figure out where.

Below, put in the names of places or professionals you can go to for help. Include their phone numbers, too! Before you say, "I don't know," let me remind you that we have this thing called Google. If you just type in your question, BOOM there's your answer. Here are some examples of things you can type in your search bar for help:

- I need help with _______________
- substance abuse counselors near me
- rehabilitation centers near me
- professional counselors and therapists near me
- support groups near me
- homeless shelters near me
- domestic violence shelters near me
- abuse shelters near me
- food bank near me

Continue on the next page!   171

NAME _______________________________

PHONE _______________________________

TYPE OF RESOURCE_______________________

____

NAME _______________________________

PHONE _______________________________

TYPE OF RESOURCE_______________________

____

NAME _______________________________

PHONE _______________________________

TYPE OF RESOURCE_______________________

____

Substance Abuse and Mental Health Services
Administration Hotline:

1-800-662-4357

T: Well, how old were you? Okay, we are going to have to go back for a little bit. I'm trying to gather all the pieces here. So you said you were at Crestwood, and then this girl ratted you out, and you got picked up and went to juvie. How old were you then?

S: Yes, I was sixteen, I believe. Yeah.

T: What was being in juvie like? What was going on when you were there? How long were you there?

S: They bring you in, and even as a juvenile, this kind of freaked me out, even as a juvenile, they bring you into a holding cell of your own. You are by yourself.

. . .

S: Three things I remember doing in there was 1) I read *Schindler's List*, 2) I studied a GED exam while I was there, and 3) this girl that I was locked up in there with, she had so many cuts all over her. She was a cutter. And she had so many that, I've never seen someone with that many cuts. And she was like fifteen. It looked like her arms were one big, huge cut callous if you will. That's how many times she had cut herself. And I remember thinking to myself, how could someone do this to themselves? And it's funny cause at the time, I wasn't thinking about how could I be doing the damage I'm doing to my own body right now because you couldn't see that damage. I could see her damage on the outside of her body, and it was appalling to me. But looking back now, my damage was just as appalling, it was just interior.

T: How were you able to get by for so long and somebody not notice and somebody not call it out?

S: I think my parents, who were still going through their divorce, were just kind of dealing with their own issues at the time, so I was kind of overlooked, plus I wasn't home much. Once I got my driver's license, I would be gone for days on end. And not come home. And they didn't really say anything about it, so I felt like I had like this kind of freedom to do whatever the hell I wanted. I think originally it started out where they trusted me. I was getting straight A's, I was a runner, I was a good kid, and then I flipped the script. And I hid it from them for a long time. And then I left home at seventeen.

Worth More

In Florence, Italy stands one of the most famous statues in the world, the statue of David. It's a seventeen-foot tall naked statue of David (the guy in the Bible who defeated Goliath) made up of marble. The artist, Michelangelo, took over two years to make the statue. One of the reasons why it's so famous is not only because of how tall it is, but it was also one of the first statues to depict emotion. A lot of people would say it's priceless.

I saw the statue. We had to wait in line for almost two hours just to get in the museum. Once you're in the museum, they tell you to be quiet for reverence of the art there. You have to be quiet for a statue! You enter this huge hallway, and the statue is way down at the other end, and the hallway is flooded with people trying to get close enough to take a good picture. That was another fifteen minutes or so. Of course, you can't touch it, but you can't even take a picture with flash. I got there, and I was like, that is one big naked man. We took our picture and left. That was it. There were some people who were super psyched to see it, and I get it, but for me, it was just a really cool experience. We went through all of that to see a priceless statue.

The crazy truth? You are even more valuable than a priceless statue. When we are dealing with addictions or struggling with big changes, it's really easy to forget our worth. Once you forget your worth, it's really easy to act below your value and accept less than what you're worth.

Don't do that!

Remember, you are worth more than a statue that millions from around the world flock to see. You're worth more because, unlike the statue, you're full of life. You have breath, blood, and a presence unlike anyone else's in the whole world. Yeah, the David might be cool, but it can't stand up and run or decide to be anything other than a statue. It can't grow or accomplish much on its own. But you can. In fact, I believe you will.

Remember Your Value

Below is a blank page. I want you to get any kind of coin and put it underneath this page. Now start shading it in. Pen, pencil, it doesn't matter. Once you're done with that, write the words "I Am Worth More" around it, underneath it, on top of it, it doesn't matter. Just write it. Now tear this page out and put it someplace where you need a reminder of that. Knowing your value will not only guide your actions, but it will also push you to something better.

T: So let's say you're talking to a group of high schoolers now. What would you say to a group of high schoolers that are on this journey, and maybe you don't know exactly where they're at, but you know they feel like they're on the outskirts, and hey, maybe drinking or doing this drug, it doesn't matter. I know I am oversimplifying it, but . . .

S: I feel like there would be so much, yet it's so hard to pull the right words out. Honestly, I think if people are going through a lot, they should really consider counseling, from a professional, not a school counselor. A professional counselor. School counselors are great. They're a great tool. They're a good asset to have.

. . .

S: Going to a school counselor, your peers might see you going there. So a lot of people don't reach out for help when they need it because they don't want their peers to know they are reaching out for help. They don't want to be singled out. They don't want people asking questions. "Oh, why were you in there? What's going on?" you know. You can't say nothing, it's like, "C'mon, man, c'mon." At the end of the day, when you're in difficult situations like that, even if you've already started using drugs, you should really consider getting professional help for it. And taking it seriously because now that I'm grown, all those people that were in my life, none of those people matter. None of those people care what I'm doing today, none of those people, what their thoughts of me or what their perceptions of me are just absolutely nothing.

Graduate Together

When the pandemic hit and the world got over the initial shock of lockdown, thoughts quickly went towards the graduating seniors of 2020. What a horrible time of life to miss out on. Not being able to walk across the stage. Some weren't able to say goodbyes to friends who were going off to college across the country. What was there to do? Nobody could change the fact that graduation was going to be a letdown, right?

Bring in LeBron James! LeBron saw the students' reactions on TikTok and other social media outlets, seniors crying and being let down about the situation. He heard and saw the cries and knew he could do something. He couldn't change quarantine, but he could influence the way students experienced graduation that year. He ended up putting together an event called "Graduate Together," pulling in stars and athletes of all kinds to speak to the graduating class and encourage them to keep going.

20.8 million students tuned in for their graduation to have President Obama to speak to them. 20.8 million students' graduation was made a little better than what the current situation was offering. The thing is, the student that convinced LeBron to put it together, the TikTok video that caught his eye, was someone who doesn't even know they were the push. All we know is that their cry for help was heard and changed the end result for so many.

Nobody can hear your cry if you don't speak up. Friends are cool to talk to, but having someone who is a professional to talk to can make all the difference. A student talking with a counselor was one of the pushes to make this book. You might not have a LeBron in your life, but you definitely have people around you that make big differences in the lives of students and others just like you. All you have to do is speak up. Cry out. It's not too late to change the direction of your ship. There will always be icebergs in our path, but we don't have to let it be our last destination or our defining one.

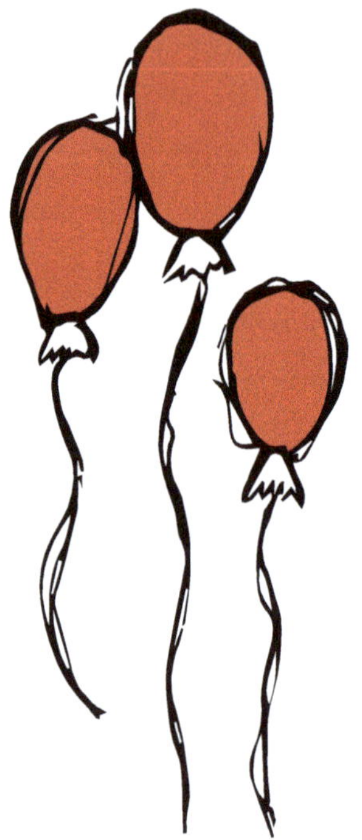

Bucket List

Write down fifty things you want to do before you kick the bucket. I have a list. You are actually reading one thing on my bucket list right now. If you write it down, you gotta do it sometime.

-
-
-
-
-
-
-
-

IF YOU JUDGE PEOPLE, YOU HAVE NO TIME TO LOVE THEM.

Mother Teresa

MORAL VALUES
Bullying and Taking the High Road

With everything that Jared has been through, he should be angry. From trying to figure out who he is by himself to being maliciously made fun of, Jared should be mad at the people around him. But he's not. Despite every hurt, name calling, or shame thrust onto him, Jared still wasn't bitter. He learned a new way to deal with the hurt around him and still love people. Jared focused on the good.

Scan the QR code to watch a message
from Terrence about

DOING GOOD

TERRENCE LEE TALLEY
DON'T
TERRENCE LEE TALLEY

Tik Tok

Here's the deal: I love TikTok. Depending on when you're reading this, TikTok is either something everyone has heard about, or this reference hasn't aged well and this book is in need of an updated reprint. No matter when you're reading this, I love TikTok because of the randomness of all the videos on the platform.

Now, if you have somehow missed what is going on in the world, or if you are in a time when TikTok has disappeared like Myspace (if you don't know that reference, just wait until some kid goes, "What's TikTok?" and then you will feel my pain), TikTok is a social media platform where people can post any video that they've created in sixty seconds or less. I love how you can see any type of video, but TikTok can analyze the videos you spend the most time on and continually provide you with content that matches your interests without you needing to search for it. Because of that, my feed is constantly full of videos of people doing acts of kindness and restoring faith in humanity.

The other day, I saw a video of a guy who wanted to help his friend who was struggling with paying the bills at his barbershop. You see him asking his friend for a haircut, and after he's done getting a fresh fade, he asks his friend, "How much does it cost?" His friend tells him it's $30. So then you see the guy take out his phone and wire his friend four thousand dollars! He begins to walk out the shop when his friend realizes what he did. "Wait a minute . . . You made a mistake." He then yells out, "No, I didn't! Byyyyyyyyeeeee!" Video done.

You are left there thinking, "I want him to be my friend." Somebody wrote in the comments on the video, "What do you do for a job? Are you rich or something?" He responded with another video basically saying that he is not rich, but the four thousand dollars you see him giving to his friend was for a car he was saving up for himself. He later went on to say that he couldn't stand to see his friend struggle doing what he loves to do, so he would rather walk to work. I was able to see what the value of friendship looks like when it is put into action.

This is what "doing good" is.

Doing good starts with what you value. This dude valued friendship above a car. A value is something you think is important in life. Your values will drive you to the kind of good you will do. ***Below are some championship trophies. Write your values on the trophies.***

Take one of the values you wrote in your trophies and explain why that matters to you.

J: Let's start with my family structure. I feel like that's where a lot of people's stories start, because family is usually where you learn most of how you cope with life and how you learn about life.

I don't. I am not a handyman whatsoever. I once had to replace a toilet ring (bet you didn't know toilets have rings), and everyone told me it was really easy. I watched the shortest YouTube video I could find (I don't have time for a video longer than five minutes), found some tools, and got to work on this "easy" project. I ended up putting my hand where the ... sewage ... was causing more sewage to spill out all over our bathroom floor. All that to say, I don't do handy work.

But, from what I've heard about building a house, it all starts with the foundation. If you don't have a good foundation, then you could end up with cracks in your walls and floors, doors that don't open or close properly, and your house sinking into the ground. I'm sure there are a lot of you who feel like Jared, and your life foundation is not very good.

When it's the foundation of our family/emotional house, you can find cracks in how you process and perceive life. For Jared, you'll see how he struggled to deal with pain, his own identity, and the people in his life. Talking with Jared, though, I was impressed by how he recognized the problem with his foundation and how that self-awareness helped him later on in life. In fact, it even helped him to help others.

You have to be aware of your foundation. A lot of us (myself included), have some cracks in the foundation of our lives, and it stops us from responding to things in a healthy way. For some, when you're put in a situation where people put you down or you're being bullied, it either makes you stay down and think less of yourself, or it'll make you want to lash out and hurt the closest thing to you.

For others, it makes it hard not to have the spotlight on you. It makes it hard to do good for the people around you, because you're constantly thinking about the good that you need for yourself. So we have to be aware of the cracks in our foundation in order to fix these issues. ***Write down some of the cracks in your foundation below.***

J: I just wish I was told that there are judgement-free people out there, and I just had to find them.

T: Did you ever feel like somebody, either at school or church… people would make you feel like you weren't accepted there? Obviously, you had that in your household, but did it happen outside of that?

J: Well, in middle school I definitely didn't feel safe at all. I mean, I've never been a very masculine person, and like that would always get the "F" slur thrown at me all the time. There was a website made of me when I was in sixth grade, made about how I was—I'm gonna use foul language because this is what the website said—it said that I was a fa**** with a man-gina that preyed on men. In sixth grade.

T: They made a website when you were in sixth grade, about you?

J: Yeah, and I had no idea what I did. I was just . . . I didn't have any friends in sixth grade, really, at school, because I was still pretty new to the public school. I was in private schools up until fourth grade. So I was still finding people to connect with, but . . . like, that . . . yeah, that really pushed me back from feeling comfortable with people.

T: How did they know this about you?

J: I don't think they really knew anything about me. That's the thing. I was just a boy that didn't like sports. I was a boy that played video games, but I didn't play like violent or sports or masculine games. I played the happy gay stuff . . .

I am not a fan of LeBron James. I am not too big into sports in general (I'm more of a movie/theatre guy), but I do follow basketball, and LeBron James has always been the enemy to my hometown team. He's too good, and he makes the game too unfair . . . in my opinion. Hence, why he's made it to the Finals a bajillion times. It's because he's the best player, who plays with all the best players, and not only that . . . Sorry. As you can see, he's a sore subject for me in the basketball world.

But, off the court, he's *the man*. In 2018, LeBron James started the I Promise school. This wasn't just any school. It's a school designed to help students who are like he was when he was growing up. He lived in a single-parent household, constantly moving, not having food or clothes, and not having any friends. Basketball was his only outlet. He eventually made some great friends and went on to skip college and play in the NBA. He never forgot those days of not having friends, a place to eat, or clothes to wear. So he started a school to provide all these things in his hometown.

At the I Promise school, students are provided with free tuition, free school uniforms, free breakfast and lunch, free transportation if you live a certain distance from the school, a free bicycle and helmet, access to a food pantry for their family, guaranteed tuition for all graduates to the University of Akron, and designated time for students to help make connections with one another. To help them make friends.

I want to go to this school, and I am a grown adult. LeBron could have easily been proud of himself for making it out of the situation he grew up in and revelled in the fact he is a millionaire (he's way more than a millionaire, but that's beside the point). He didn't though. He took his experiences and made something good from it.

The reason I am writing this journal is because I had bad experiences in school and felt like I couldn't express my feelings. This is what doing good is. We all experience bad things, and it's really easy to get pulled into resentment, anger, and hate, but that doesn't help you or anyone else. When we do good, it feels good. LeBron established something that will impact thousands of students for years to come. Hopefully this journal will find its way into the hands of students who really need it. Doing good always leaves an impact on others—I promise.

Just hearing Jared's story made me ask the question to myself: how would I have helped Jared? What could I have done to help? As much as I would have loved to go around and start throat-punching all the kids involved, it wouldn't have helped. Just telling someone about what is going on is definitely a start, but what else would I have done? *What would you do? Write it down, people! There are so many people like Jared, and others in different situations, that need your good in the world. So write it down on this page.*

T: What would you say, going through your whole story, what would you say if you were talking to someone who's thirteen or fourteen right now? Someone sitting there reading your story, and they're struggling. What would you want to say to them?

J: I know this is cliché, but it truly does get better. And I think it's also great to know that there are people that have your same story or parts of your story, and there are people that understand your story. And I personally think that's such a beautiful thing. If you don't feel like you can find those people, there's definitely people out there. You just have to be patient and find them.

Imagine getting shot because you want to go to school. Malala Yousafzai grew up in Pakistan, and when the Taliban came into her country, they wanted to stop the education of girls. They began attacking all the girls' schools in the country. At the age of eleven years old, Malala gave a speech defying the Taliban. She called, "How dare the Taliban take away my basic right to education?" It did not go over very well with the Taliban. Also at the age of eleven, she began blogging for a British news station (under a different name in order to hide her identity).

Malala spoke out about the right for all women to have access to fair education. She took action. She was so well known, she won the International Children's Peace Prize and the Pakistan's National Youth Peace Prize—all at thirteen years old!

The Taliban eventually issued a death threat on her life. Malala wasn't worried about her life, though she was afraid for her father. Her family was sure that the group wouldn't hurt a child. But on October 9th, when Malala was just fifteen years old, a gunman jumped on her bus and shot her in the head. She was rushed to the hospital, where she was placed in critical condition. She was then flown to England, where she eventually recovered from her brain injuries.

Malala now lives in the United Kingdom, because it is still unsafe for her to return home. But this has made her want to speak out even more. At sixteen, she spoke in front

of the United Nations, focusing on education and women's rights. She urged all the world leaders to change their policies. Malala has accomplished so much and overcame the worst form of hate, and she still manages to do good for all women. When asked about her experiences, she has been quoted saying, "The terrorists thought that they would change our aims and stop our ambitions, but nothing changed in my life except this: weakness, fear, and hopelessness died. Strength, power, and courage were born."

Let weakness, fear, and hopelessness die in all of us, so the courage to do good will be unstoppable.

Ummm that's it. Draw an outline of your hand. Color it in if you want!

YOUR IMPERFECTIONS MAKE YOU **BEAUTIFUL,** THEY MAKE YOU WHO **YOU ARE.**

Demi Lovato

YOUR REFLECTION

Self-Image and Seeing the Real You

When you think of body image, you usually don't think of guys too often. Blake, though, made me see things a little differently. During the interview, I caught myself saying "Wow" many times. Read about his story and see how the way he looked at himself spread to other parts of who he is.

Too Many Feedback Forms

Recently, I received a feedback form about an assembly I did. It wasn't good. Now I'll admit, I didn't read the part where they specifically said what they were looking for during the assembly. It usually says the same thing, but we all know what happens when you assume (or if you haven't heard the saying, look it up). Anyway, the principal filled out the form for the assembly he saw. It ripped me to shreds, and it was very thorough in doing so. I have done numerous school assemblies in my speaking career. Over ten years! In those ten years, I have received two feedback forms that totally took my confidence away . . . and I remember both vividly.

Feedback forms stink. How many people have rated your mistakes? How many people have rated the things you thought you were good at? Rated things you can't change about yourself? Rated your looks based on their definition of what looks good?

Feedback is good for things that require a level of skill. It allows for the correction of something that is potentially harmful to you or others. It has to be done in a healthy way, though. A way that encourages and brings redemption. Feedback is unnecessary, I think, when it comes to the unchangeable—things like your looks and your value. It's always the most negative feedback that sticks, isn't it? You constantly replay or reread the words that caused the most damage. You know how to stop that negative replay crap? You replay the positive truth.

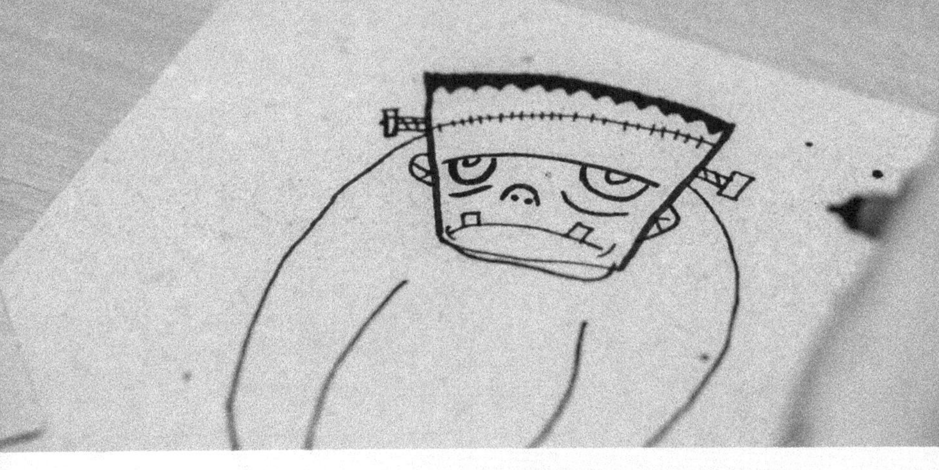

B: I've had body image issues since I was five or six years old. I remember being in kindergarten, and I've always had a big head. A big head and very long head. So I remember being five years old and getting made fun of. My classmates would say, "He looks like Frankenstein." And I remember feeling really badly about that, and at five or six years old, really being aware that my body was not pleasing to other people. They made fun of me, and as a five-year-old, that's a lot to process.

It's a Phenomenon!

Let's say you buy a new, blue car. Once you start driving it, you start to notice every time you see the same type of car. You not only notice it everywhere, but you also start noticing how some people have the better model and even if they don't, you feel like yours is in the worst condition out of all of them. Your car doesn't seem as good anymore.

This happens to all of us at some point. It's that awful feeling of jealousy and embarrassment. And once you focus on it too much, it's everywhere, all the time.

For Blake, it was his body. Everyone has one, but Blake thought all the others were better than his. For others, it's noticing how pretty (or good-looking) everyone else is but how ugly you are—and everybody seems to be constantly talking about beauty, reminding you of this. For some, it's a college you wanted to get into, and now everyone you know is getting into it except you. In my case, everyone else seemed to be going to college, and I wasn't. You focus on something for a moment, and all of sudden it's everywhere.

There is a combination of two things going on here. It's the Baader-Meinhof phenomenon and comparison disease (I don't know if the comparison thing is real, but it sure sounds like it). Baader-Meinhof phenomenon is when your awareness of something increases, and because you're paying more attention to it, it seems like it's happening more. In the example, it makes you think that more people are buying the same car as you, but in reality, it's just that you are more aware

of it now. Comparison disease, according to me, is when you start feeling good about something, but then your brain attacks that feeling and begins to tell you how something or someone else is better.

You mix those two together, and you have a deadly dose of rampant comparisons. It makes you think that you will always come in second, or in some cases last, to everyone else. I hate that feeling, and I want to punch it in the throat! DON'T LIVE YOUR LIFE IN CONSTANT COMPARISON! It adds stress and takes the joy out of your life. You deserve more.

Scan the QR code to watch a message from Terrence about

CHANGING YOUR STARE

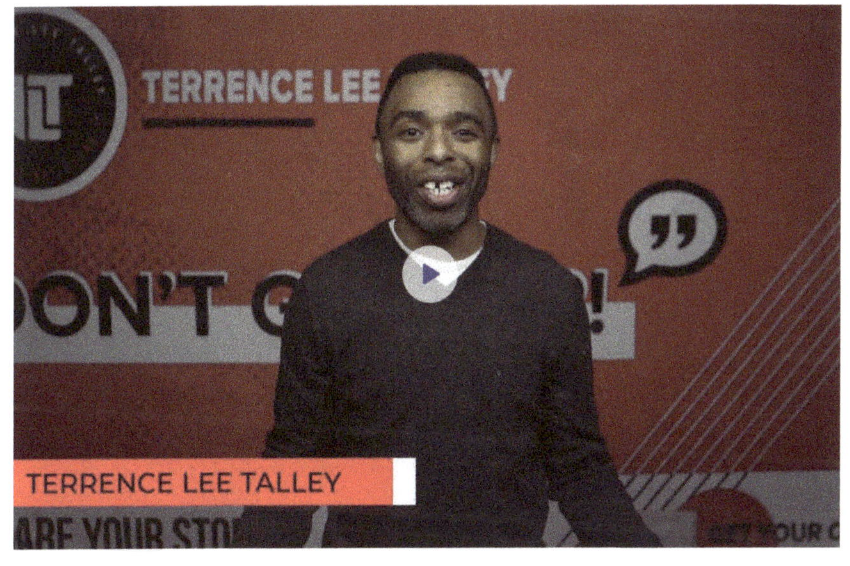

Cross that Bull Out!

Okay, we gotta get this . . . stuff out of your vision. See the two columns on the next page? In one column, I want you to write all the things you compare yourself to and the things that stress you out. Then in the other column, write all of the things you are proud of about yourself.

If you say you are not proud of anything, so help me I will pull this car over and make someone else write it for you and then hug you afterwards (for those of you who are introverts, this could be a really serious threat).

Once you've done that, next to all the things that stress you out or make you feel not-good-enough, write some doable actions you can take to ease some of that stress or get yourself less focused on that comparison. Then scratch out the things in the left column as you address them, and I mean really scratch. Soon, you'll only be focusing on the things you should be focusing on. Like how awesome you are! You may not be all the things you want to be, but what you actually are is better than all that.

Comparisons
Points of Pride

B: You know, there was a girl that I really liked, that I really gushed over. Everybody knew that I liked her. And she was really nice to me. Every other girl would just make fun of me for liking them. But this was probably seventh or eighth grade, and there was this girl that I really really liked, and I remember we were literally sitting outside of school. My dad was a teacher, and I was waiting for him to finish up, and she was waiting for her parents. We were just talking, and I remember her saying to me, "Blake, I don't want to embarrass you at the dance tonight. Please don't ask me to dance."

T: What does that do to you?

B: Here's the thing. My self-esteem was so low, I thought she was being nice. I was like, "Thank you for doing that." I thought, she doesn't want to embarrass me, so she must care about me or respect me.

On meeting people in online chatrooms:

B: The thought was, I'm never gonna get this in real life, because of who I am. So I will accept this cheap substitute, because the cheap substitute is better than nothing.

When Blake told me this part of his story, I was shocked. I couldn't believe that 1) someone would actually say that to him and 2) he was glad she did.

The way you see yourself physically and emotionally has a huge effect on what you are going to put up with. I wish I could instantly change how you see yourself and respond to the world around you. It's hard to break through that wall that's blocking you from accepting yourself, the wall that keeps you trapped in a room of fear and stress. I might not be able to knock down that wall for you, but I can definitely help you change what's on those walls.

On the next page, write out things you like about yourself or things that you have overcome. Next, tear out each thing you wrote and tape it on your ceiling, mirror, or literal walls in your room. This way, you are telling yourself what to focus on until you're ready to knock that wall down and actually believe it for yourself.

Use this page

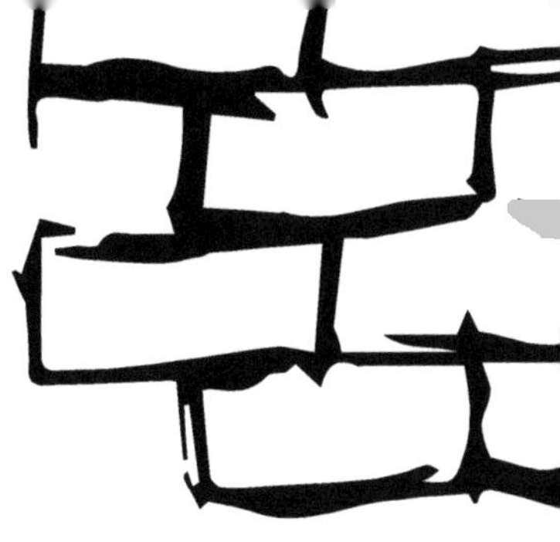

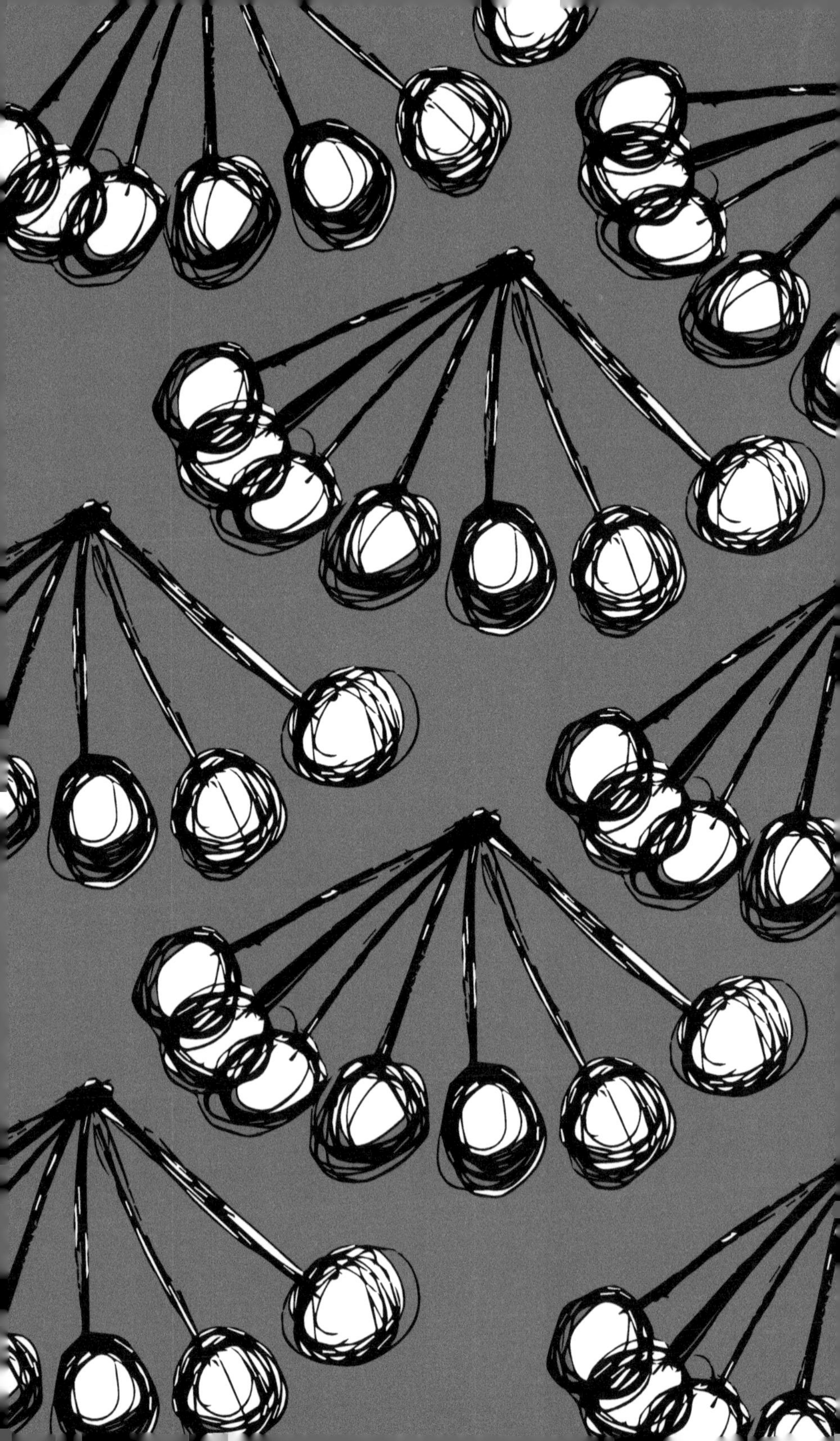

B: I feel like there is this unhealthy pendulum swing, where we went from 'You have to be real thin and you have to look like an athlete or a model' to this fat-acceptance all the way over here that says, 'It's okay to be 550 pounds.' And I'm sitting here like, 'No, it's not, you're gonna die.' It's just not healthy. Like, it's not good to make fun of, or to mock, those people. But if we could encourage the process of being healthy instead of the result, then we'd have a lot more healthy people.

Not the Bad Guy After All

Have you ever heard a song for the first time and not liked it, but then after a few more listens you're like, "This is actually good"? That's how I felt about "Bad Guy" by Billie Eilish. At first, it sounded really weird to me (I know what you're thinking, but it's not because I am old). The more I listened to the song, though, I actually liked its truly original sound. This made me want to look into Billie Eilish's music more and see who she is. Not only have I become a fan of her music, but I've also become a fan of her story. The clothes she wears actually tell a lot about her story. She has dealt a lot with body image issues, and because of that she wears baggy clothes. Now, there is a lot more to her story and I don't have the space to go over it all, but it comes down to that one central idea: how hard it is not to like yourself.

She did this short film called "Not My Responsibility," in which she talks about how people have all these different opinions about her and how there is no way she can please everyone. In the film, Billie asks whether her value is based off of our perception of her. She ends it by saying that our opinion of her is not her responsibility. Meaning: it doesn't matter what you think about her or her body, because it's her own business. She's going to shut out all those other opinions and focus on her opinion of herself. Does she still struggle with body issues? Yes. She explains that it's a fight for her every time she looks in the mirror. Does it mean she is going to be okay because she's mastered the art of blocking out the

opinions of the world? No. This is hard. Self-image is so hard. I would even venture to say that for others (and maybe Billie as well), it may be good to go talk with a counselor to help ease that struggle.

So what does it mean? It means it's a great start. It's hard to change our focus, but it can be done. Plus, what's most impressive is that her drive to push out those other opinions actually inspired others to do the same—and it actually saved a girl's life.

A teenage girl named Marissa was surprised by Billie on a talk show. Marissa was talking about how at just sixteen, she had to take care of her mother and brother despite not being in a good place in terms of mental health. She explained that there were days when she would just go to her room and cry because of how badly she wanted to give up, but then she would put on a Billie Eilish song. The music reminded her of how Billie is so honest about her struggles but still moves forward, and it inspired her to do the same. Next thing you know, in comes Billie! Marissa instantly started crying (me as well). Getting the chance to meet the person she admired and was inspired by was a big deal.

I don't know what happened to Marissa once the cameras were off, but I am sure it was a moment that she will never forget and has changed her life forever. Marissa didn't just love Billie's music, but she loved her story as well, and it changed her life. Billie, as far as I know, was just trying to make herself healthy and focus on her own opinions of herself. Yet, changing her focus helped Marissa (and countless others I'm sure) to do the same.

I don't know if it's body issues, people's opinions, social media, news stories, or just the world around you pulling you down, but I do know this: when we focus on the negative, it will continue to bring us down. You deserve to be lifted up! It's true, we have work to do within ourselves, and it will take time, but it is the most important challenge. Be kind to yourself, and remember your self-worth, because you are awesome and important!

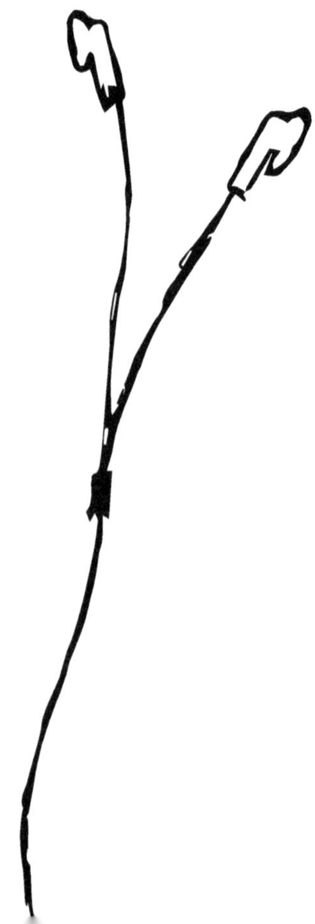

Write down something that someone said to you today. If it wasn't a good thing they said, then write it down and scratch it out.

BEING **GOOD**
TO PEOPLE

IS A
WONDERFUL
LEGACY TO
LEAVE BEHIND.

Taylor Swift

IT MATTERS

The Impact of Abuse and Hope

Brielle has had many moments that she could look back on and ask if they truly made a difference. When hearing about her family and how her mom's struggles put Brielle and her sister in danger, I kept on thinking how strong she was. She was strong for herself and for her sister, and I know it made a world of difference for both of them. When you read her story about protecting her sister, remember that she was only nine years old at the time.

I Fought a Mountain

I once almost died on top of a mountain. Okay, that may be a little exaggerated. It's more like I was almost hospitalized on top of a mountain for nothing.

This is how it went down. I was asked to speak at a summer camp in Colorado for two weeks. I was super excited. I would be able to see mountains, go on hikes if I wanted, and basically just enjoy being in the Rockies (which is another name for Colorado, I think). I got picked up from the airport and began a two-hour-plus drive to the camp. I am a narcoleptic, so I instantly fell asleep in the car. The first week of the camp, I was having a blast. Playing basketball, watching out for bears (another story for another book), and playing night games. Between all the games and speaking, the week went pretty fast.

When the weekend hit, it was totally a different story. No kids were around. No basketball. No night games. No nothing. Of course, this camp is in the middle of nowhere, so there wasn't anything to do. There was a movie theater in Denver, though, which was about two hours away. I am a big movie fan, and I had nothing better to do, so I figured why not see a movie that Friday night? So I took my two hour drive down a hill to the theater and then back up the hill to the camp. I did this on Friday night, Saturday night, and Sunday night. My weekend was filled with driving up and down that huge hill. Monday came around, and it was the start of the next camp. Monday, I was feeling great, ready to rock this

camp. Tuesday, I was feeling a little off and needed to take naps during the day. Wednesday came, and I couldn't even get out of bed. My head was killing me, my nose was stuffed, and my body just hurt. I was thinking I couldn't speak that night. I couldn't even make it through the day.

The camp director came to my room, took one look at me, and said, "Oh no. I totally forgot to tell you. Let's go to the hospital." Forgot to tell me what? At that point, I really didn't care what he forgot to tell me, I just needed to go to the hospital. We got there, and right away the doctor said, "Yeah. He has elevation sickness." As it turns out, what the director forgot to tell me was that the big hill that took two-plus-hours both ways was actually a MOUNTAIN. This mountain was over 10,000 miles above sea level! So every time I went down and up the mountain, my body wasn't able to adjust that fast to the change in elevation. Throw in the fact that I don't drink a lot of water (I know I have to work on that), and this completely wrecked me. I instantly was put on IV and was given an oxygen tank. The director came in, looked at me, and said, "You don't have to speak tonight if you don't want to."

Of course, I am a tough dude. I couldn't wimp out just because I couldn't breathe and my body felt like death. I had to speak that night. Let me tell you, THAT WAS THE WORST NIGHT OF SPEAKING I'VE EVER HAD! I constantly stopped to catch my breath. I was sweating. I felt like I was going to throw up. It wasn't good, and I struggled for the rest of the week. Friday came, and I was ready to get off that mountain and go home.

As I was picking up, the director came over and said, "You were here for a reason. The story you told on Wednesday night led a girl to come clean about the abuse that was going on in her house. We're getting her help. She said the story was exactly what she needed to hear to encourage her." When I was in the midst of speaking that Wednesday, feeling like every minute was pure crap, I asked myself, "What am I doing? This is not worth it." Looking back on that day and the other times I fought "mountains," it all seemed like the fight wasn't worth it in the moment, but my fight is never just *my* fight. The truth is, I've been fighting for that student and many others. My fight mattered to someone else, even when I didn't know it.

Scan the QR code to watch a message
from Terrence about why

WHAT YOU DO MATTERS

Everybody has those moments when it seems like what you're doing doesn't matter, but it could be days, months, or even years before you realize that it did make a difference. ***In the glasses on the next page, write some of those moments. Even if you think it only made a small difference, write that down, too. Those small moments may be bigger than you think.***

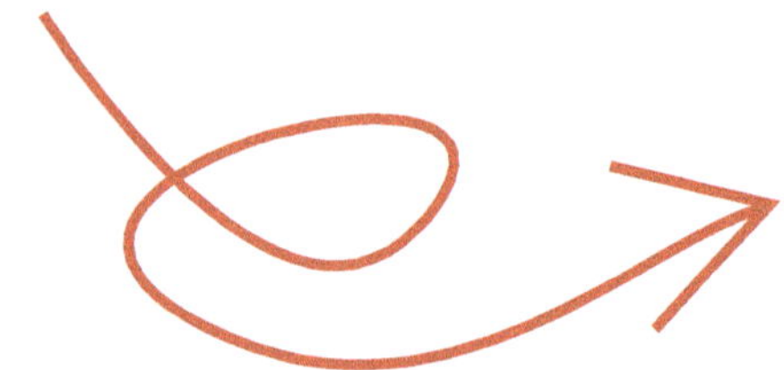

B: It was kind of me and my sister against the world, really. I had to grow up really fast to take care of her, make sure she got her homework done, make sure I got my homework done. I made sure she was safe, that was the big thing. Keeping her away from my mom was a big one, too. I specifically remember a moment where my mom was angry, for whatever reason. She was angry a lot. She went after my sister, and all I could think about was that I couldn't let her hurt my sister.

. . .

B: I think my little sister must have been talking back or something, you know, something little kids do. And she just wasn't happy about it, and so they were fighting. My mom was yelling at her, and I told her to stop. My sister ran into her room, and my mom pushed me onto the couch and went after my sister. And that was the moment when I was like, "I have to do something." So I followed, and my mom had a hand raised, and I stepped between them. I stared her down until she walked away. She gave up and decided it wasn't worth it.

"She went after my sister, and all I could think about was that I couldn't let her hurt my sister."

Not Without You

Responsible people make the world go around. We all have to be responsible for something at some point in our lives. That's part of growing up, but there are those people that feel responsible for everything and everyone. I am not that person. Give me my role, my people, and I'll get it done. I don't need the whole plan. I am not going to worry about everyone else's role and the job they do unless I have to. I don't go searching for responsibility (and I'm sure there are some of you that don't either).

But there are also people out there who love responsibility. There's always that person who wants to be in charge during group projects. They might say things like, "I just like things done a certain way," or, "Nobody else will do it," but these people deep down inside know they like the responsibility. That's a great thing! Responsible people make the world go 'round. Thing is, it can be really frustrating when you don't think anybody cares or notices what you do. That could be for big things and small things. It can almost seem like you're being taken advantage of.

My older daughter, Gracie, always takes care of her younger sister, Cece. She makes lunches for her, gets her toothbrush out for her, and will even fight for something Cece wants over something she wants. Gracie loves being responsible for her. On the other hand, though, that responsibility is one of her biggest frustrations and heartbreak. Cece does take advantage of it sometimes. She'll complain about the lunch her sister made for her, and this kills Gracie. So we know we have to continue to encourage Gracie and give her praise. Her taking care of Cece often helps my wife and me. So we won't tell her to stop taking care of her sister, and we let her know that we appreciate her.

No matter if you like being responsible for a lot of things or if you only take care of the things that are asked of you, I want you to know that I appreciate it. Whatever it is you are responsible for, it wouldn't be taken care of without you, so thank you for that.

Remember the Sticky Notes

Brielle was responsible for taking care of her sister at a very early age. I am sure her sister noticed it and appreciated it. I don't know if it's the same way with you, but I want you to remember that you are appreciated.

Get some sticky notes, and write one thing down on one sticky note you're responsible for that you don't think anybody notices. Put it on this page and underneath it, write this: I am appreciated. *Do that as many times as you need to. Remember that for each of the things you write down, I and others reading this appreciate what you do. It wouldn't have been done that way without you. You are doing a great job.*

*Brielle talks with Terrence about her tattoo,
a memorial for her mom and best friend.*

B: A couple months after she had moved out, she drove herself to the hospital, because I think she realized how sick she was getting. I think she realized how much she wanted to change and wanted to stay. So she drove herself to the hospital, and I think she was there for maybe a month and a half. She had sclerosis in her liver, scar tissue, anorexia – because she never ate anything, she just drank vodka and that was about it. She was depressed, and there were just so many things that they couldn't fix. Because she was too light. She was five-foot-one and weighed eighty or ninety pounds. So, she didn't have enough body weight for them to do a liver transplant or anything like that. So it was just us, watching my mom slowly pass away for those two months that she was in the hospital.

My sister never really went into the hospital room, because, you know, she was afraid of all the tubes and the machines and everything that was basically keeping her alive. So a lot of the visits were just me and my mom, while my dad watched my sister in the waiting room. That was a big thing, just sitting there and talking to her, and she couldn't talk back to me.

"That was a big thing, just sitting there and talking to her, and she couldn't talk back to me."

This is Going to Hurt

Here are some things I don't look forward to doing: cleaning the bathroom, going to new people's houses, walking and driving over high bridges, writing for long periods of time (I've been working on this section for three hours now), dealing with big needles at the doctor's office. These are all things I don't like, but I know that I am going to have to do them.

Something I recently had to do was take the COVID-19 test. It was awful. If you don't know, or maybe it has changed by the time you're reading this, it is a test where they stick a really long cotton swab up your nose to the point where it feels like they are touching your brain. I did not look forward to doing that for obvious reasons. The whole day before I took the test was the worst, because all day I was worrying about how I was going to have someone push my boogers into my cerebellum. I got to the place an hour beforehand to get in early. Right before they stuck it in there, they tried to explain to me what they were about to do. I was so nervous leading up to it that I read everything about the test and how far they were going to go up my nose. I didn't need her to explain it to me; I just needed her to do it. I psyched myself up, and they dove in.

That's usually how I go about everything I dread doing. I know I need to research what I am getting into and then get it over with. Just get through it as quickly as possible. This helps me. I know this strategy has gotten me through plenty of stuff before, and I use my past to reassure myself that I'll get through the next difficult thing.

How do you get through the unavoidable? *In the middle of the next page, I want you to cut out a square with some scissors (remember what I told you about watching out for your fingers). As you are doing it, think of some things that help you get through tough moments. If you don't have a way, then use this time to think of a new way. After you get done cutting the square out, write underneath it: I will get through. You can always come back to remind yourself how you got through something before.*

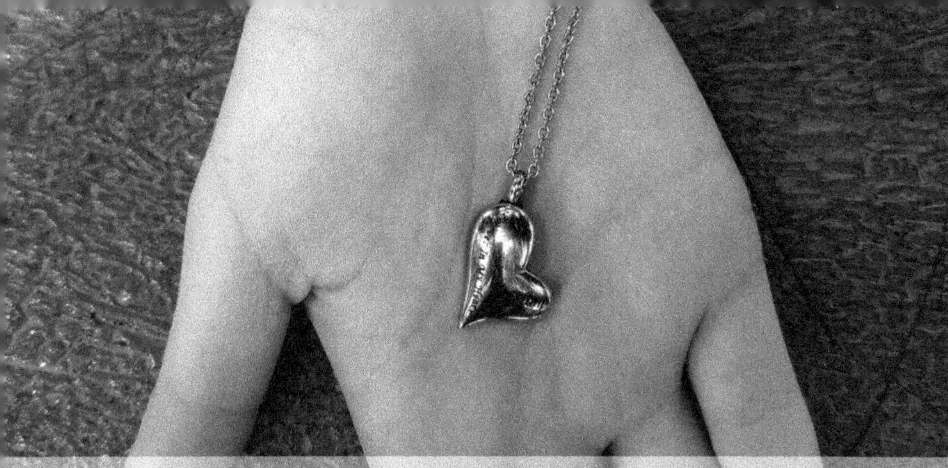

Brielle's necklace: a reminder of her mom. "Even though life was tough, we still had good times and I still love and miss her."

T: If you were to take one sentence to describe your past, what would it be?

B: I look at it like... kind of like going on a really hard hike. Because you get the down-hills, the easy stuff, the pretty views, but then there are things that happen that you don't expect. You get storms, up-hills, scrapes, bruises, and you never really know what's going to happen. For me, my past was like that, but like walking without a guide.

. . .

B: My past doesn't make me an ugly person. I'm growing up, and part of doing that is realizing that I can find myself beautiful and not feel bad about it. That was a big thing.

T: Brielle, you're my hero. You have such an amazing story. A story of not just surviving abuse, but also doing something with it. And the fact that you took care of your sister in the midst of everything that was going on... that's huge. It says a lot about your responsibility, and what you did with it.

Losing an Arm on a Hike

Aron Ralston was hiking in the canyons of Utah. This is what he loved to do, going hiking in extreme places. This day was no different. As he was crossing an opening in the canyon, he slipped and fell 100 feet into a crevice. Not only was it a far fall, but also an 800-pound boulder came down with him and trapped his arm between the boulder and the wall. After pulling and squirming for an hour or so, he thought he'd wait for someone to come and get him. Three hours turned into eleven. Eleven hours turned into a full day. One day turned into three. After five days (127 hours), he knew no one was coming. He had to get out by himself.

Knowing what he had to do, he broke his arm (this is where it gets gross) and proceeded to cut off his arm with a dull knife. To make matters even worse, he still had to hike out of the canyon, and the nearest paved road was twenty miles away. But he made it.

This was probably the worst hiking experience of all time. They eventually made a movie about his experience called 127 Hours starring James Franco. He was asked about how it felt watching the movie, and he said it was surreal. The thing that he thought really captured his experience was the scenes of him being with his family and friends. He said that was what that got him through. A crew went back to survey the area where he was trapped, found his arm, cremated it, and brought it back to him. He said that he took the ashes,

went back to where everything happened, and left the ashes there because that's where they belong. He had another life now, the life of a survivor.

I hope none of you are forced to do anything that drastic. I know there are a lot of you who are going through some horrific moments. Or maybe you're not, and that's a great thing. But everyone will have to go through something unpleasant eventually. Sometime you go through it by yourself, but that doesn't mean you are alone.

On this page, write down the names of three people who have overcome great odds to get to where they are. Then write down one thing that inspires you about each of their stories. It can be someone you know, an athlete, a celebrity, your teacher (I see all you teachers out there), an author, or even a fictional character. Whoever it is, learn their story so that when you're striving to overcome something, or maybe you feel like no one sees your hard work, you remember there are people out there that have made it. So can you.

It's In Your Heart

I am no one special. Now, that doesn't mean people don't love me. It doesn't mean I am less than other people or that I have no special purpose. When I say, "I am no one special," I mean that everything I've done could be done by other people. Did I have to do a lot of work? Yup. Did I have to get myself out of my comfort zone? Oh yeah. Did I have to sacrifice time and money? You bet. Did I encounter failure, heartbreak, frustration, and moments when I wanted to give up? You have no idea! People always ask, "How do you get to do the things you do? How'd you get to where you are?"

Honestly, the answer is heart.

When I think about that, it reminds me of a story I heard. In this small town, there was a town square where everyone came to marvel at a man with the perfect heart. They were in awe of how shiny it looked. The people excitedly pointed out how smooth and steady his heartbeat was. Even this man was impressed by his own heart. In almost a trance, one person said, "It's perfect. It's the most beautiful heart I've ever seen." The man, feeling affirmed and full of pride, said, "I suppose it is." That's when someone in the back yelled out, "That's not true!" The crowd turned toward the back to see a young boy pulling an older man behind him. He made it up to the front and placed the older man right next to the man with the "perfect" heart. The famous man looked at the grungy-looking guy with the dirty coat and unshaven face, and he asked, "Who is this?" The young boy said, "He has the most beautiful heart I've ever seen." "Oh really?" the man replied. "Yeah, show them," the boy urged the older gentleman. The older man reached in his coat and pulled out this heart that had scars on it, pieces that looked like they were stitched together, and even some areas where pieces of other people's heart were sewn to his heart. The people were confused as they looked at it. The man with the "perfect" heart looked with disgust at this strange heart and asked, "Why do you think this is beautiful?" The boy looked at the older man with a smile, and he smiled back at him. "It's simple," the boy said, "this man has scars where people hurt him and some places where it seems like he hurt himself. Those other pieces where there are bits of other people's hearts came from times when he gave them a piece of his heart and they gave him a piece of theirs." The man looked at it judgingly and asked, "This is what beauty looks like to you?" "Yeah," the boy said, "with all those scars, stitches, and other people's pieces, there is a story—a story of loss, hurt, trauma, and love. I know this, because he told me and showed me. Because of that, he has the most beautiful heart I've ever seen."

This is what I try to do with my life. When I share my stories of hurt, trauma, and love, it helps give it all a sense of purpose. I put my heart into telling my stories, because

I know it will help at least one person. When people hear and see my heart, they will see the hope in it. If sharing my heart has given me joy, purpose, and hope, then I want you to have the same.

Your journey of telling your story doesn't end here. Continue on with writing it out, acting it out, and making a clear picture of your story to share with others. Will it be easy? No. Will you encounter heartbreak? Probably. Will your story be a perfect happily ever after? Nope, but beauty doesn't come from perfection. It comes from truth and love.

Share it when you can, so others will know that there is beauty in their story, too.

One Last Thing

On the next page is a picture of a heart. I want you to make it into your heart. Where are your scars, and what did they come from? Whose pieces of heart do you have? Who has your pieces? Color it in, and then look at the beauty in your story. In your heart.

EXTRAS

Okay. We've covered *a lot* in this book. Maybe you feel like you need some more space to journal and work through your thoughts. That's why we've added the following pages for you!

CPSIA information can be obtained
at www.ICGtesting.com
Printed in the USA
BVHW020312311220
596702BV00006B/21